HUMANKIND HACKS

D0892585

MAN HACKS

Copyright © Summersdale Publishers Ltd, 2017

Illustrations by Kostiantyn Fedorov

Research by Agatha Russell

Summersdale Publishers Ltd
46 West Street
Chichester
West Sussex
PO19 1RP
UK

www.summersdale.com

Printed and bound in Croatia

ISBN: 978-1-78685-192-5

Substantial discounts on bulk quantities of Summersdale books are available to corporations, professional associations and other organisations. For details contact general enquiries: telephone: +44 (0) 1243 771107, fax: +44 (0) 1243 786300 or email: enquiries@summersdale.com

HUMANKIND HACKS

Handy Hints to Make Life Easier

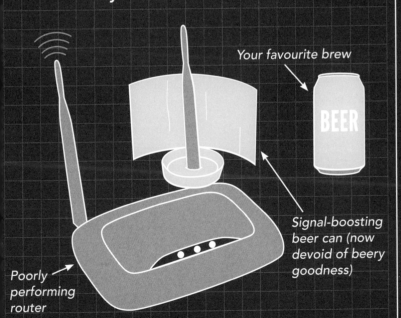

Your favourite brew

BEER

Signal-boosting
beer can (now
devoid of beery
goodness)

Poorly
performing
router

Dan Marshall

Over **130** amazing hacks inside!

CONTENTS

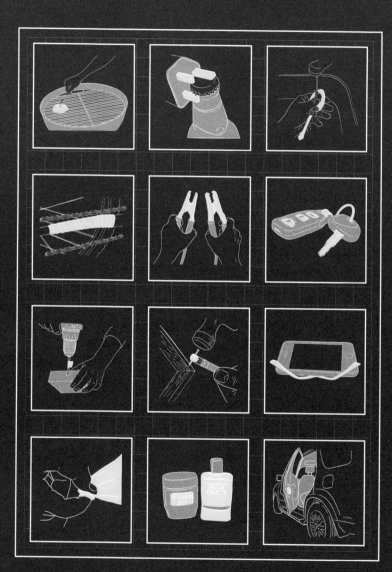

INTRODUCTION

Welcome to *Man Hacks* [Hu Kind], the book for men [and women] who want to make their lives easier by doing less and winning more. No matter if you're already a full-blown Bear Grylls outdoorsman [or outdoors woman] know your full Windsor from your Nicky Knot or are one project away from being a DIY master [or mistress] you'll find new ways to man up [or do better] in this handy volume. We've got all the bases covered: food, drink, fashion, fixing things – as well as a healthy dose of survival shortcuts and gadget hacks to top things off. Simply flick to the relevant section, check out the diagram and hey presto, you're hacking. Whatever you're doing, *HuMan Kind Hacks* will see you right.

FOOD
HACKS

What is there to hack, you say? It's food – you cook it and you eat it. If you haven't got the hang of that by now then you need more than a book for help. But even if you've got your culinary skills down, there are always ways of making things quicker, smarter and tastier.

NO-MESS CUPCAKE

Here's a sweet hack to start the proceedings (yes, it is OK to start with dessert, you're a grown man!). Cupcakes are delicious, but the amount of icing on them can be prohibitive, especially if more of it ends up in your moustache than in your mouth - not a good look. This simple hack shows you how to avoid this.

Take your cupcake and cut it in half horizontally, then just place the top icing side down onto the base. Now you can have your cake and eat it too.

Flipped cupcake

Icing safely nestled in sponge

PRESERVE YOUR HERBS

Any guy worth his salt in the kitchen knows that fresh herbs turn a good meal into a great one. But if, like many people, you choose to buy your fresh herbs from the supermarket, you can often find you simply have too much. Don't be wasteful and throw the extra herbs in the bin – preserve them with this hack.

Grab an ice cube tray and fill each little cube section almost to the top with olive oil. Next, chop up your excess herbs, then proceed to add them to the oil in the tray. Place them in the freezer and you are left with handy cubes that can be defrosted for the next time you need a handful of herbs.

Petrified parsely

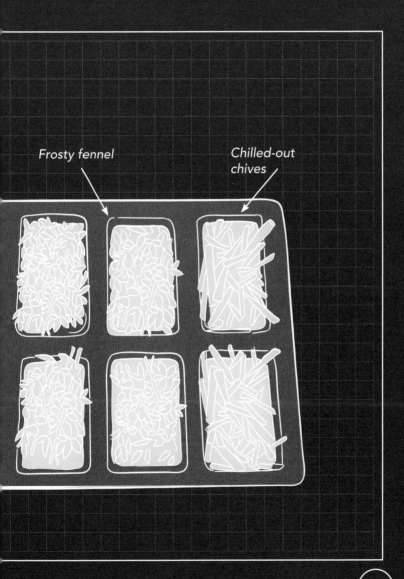

Frosty fennel

Chilled-out chives

SPICE UP YOUR BBQ COALS

Nothing can compare to cooking over hot coals for that awesome slow-cooked, smoky flavour. (Less so when you've squirted half a bottle of lighter fluid on your barbecue.)

For a natural flavour boost to your coals, place a few sprigs of fresh herbs on top once you have them glowing. Rosemary, basil, sage, thyme, mint, fresh garlic, bay leaves and fennel will all infuse your food with flavour.

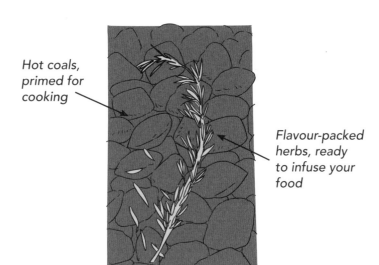

Hot coals, primed for cooking

Flavour-packed herbs, ready to infuse your food

NON-STICK GRILL

Sticking with the subject of outdoor cooking – or non-sticking, in this instance – here's another hack to improve your BBQ experience. If you're working with a narrow-gauge grill you might find food will stick quite readily. Here's how to stop it.

Slice a whole onion in two, stick a fork into the curved side and carefully rub the sliced end onto the grill. Once the grill is covered in onion you are ready to start your non-stick cooking!

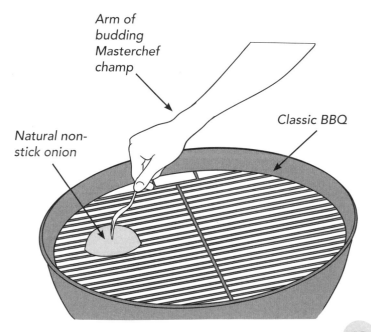

Arm of budding Masterchef champ

Classic BBQ

Natural non-stick onion

PERFECT PANCAKES AND BACON

Do you like pancakes? Do you like bacon? If the answer is yes, chances are you will love this hack. (If the answer is no, move on quickly.) Pancakes with bacon and maple syrup is an American breakfast classic, but traditionally bacon is served on top of the pancakes, which can compromise your chances of achieving the perfect bacon-to-pancake mouthful. This hack solves the problem.

Prepare your batter, cook your bacon and then carefully pour your pancake mix over and along the length of the rasher. What you get is pancake heaven.

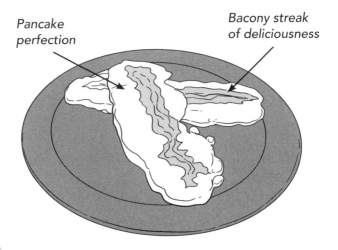

Pancake perfection

Bacony streak of deliciousness

SMART SANDWICH

If you're a fan of machine-sliced meat and other foods that come in vaguely disc-shaped portions, here's a hack to help your filling actually reach the edges of your bread.

It's basic geometry – make your circles squares by slicing them in half and lining up the straight edges with the outside edges of your bread. Even better, tear up the slices and arrange them evenly. Your sandwich is now infinitely more edible!

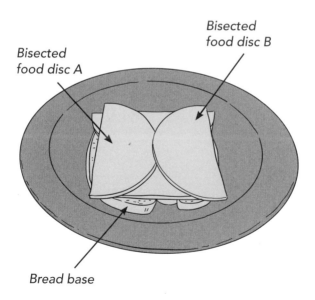

Bisected
food disc B

Bisected
food disc A

Bread base

STEAK CHECK

If you're cooking steak for your dinner guests there's no avoiding asking them how they'd like it cooked. It's the least you can do for such an expensive cut of meat (let alone your fancy friends). So here's how to get it right.

For rare steak, the texture of the meat should resemble the softness of your cheek; for medium, touch your chin; for well done (groan!), touch your forehead. If they want anything in between, remind them that this is your house, not a Michelin-starred restaurant.

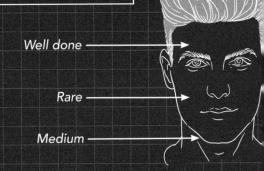

Well done —

Rare —

Medium —

Imperceptible aroma →

Perfectly cooked steak

Your most expensive pan (only the best for your meat)

PERFECT PIZZA SLICE

Put the pizza wheel down and step away from the giant kitchen knife – despite what you might think, these items are not effective implements when cutting a pizza. What you need is a pair of scissors.

Slicing through a well-baked crust is no longer a chore, and you'll also be able to cut cleanly through the centre without pulling off any toppings along the way. Perfect pizza in a snip!

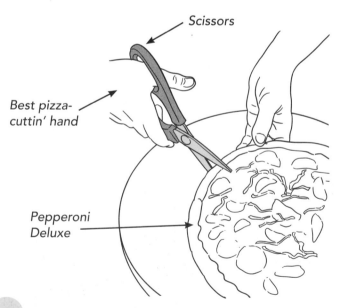

Scissors

Best pizza-cuttin' hand

Pepperoni Deluxe

PIMP YOUR TACOS

If you're a fan of Mexican food (if not, why not?!) here's how to get the most out of your taco.

First, make sure you bought corn tortillas. Preheat your oven to 190 degrees and grab a cupcake tray (don't worry, you can also use them for Yorkshire puddings, so they're worth a buy) and turn it upside down. Take your tortillas, spray them lightly with oil and place in between the mounds to make a kind of plus shape. Place them in the oven to crisp and when they're slightly brown remove and fill your taco 'bowls' generously with more filling than you could ever hope to do otherwise.

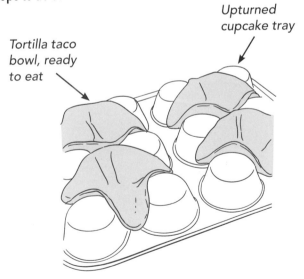

Upturned cupcake tray

Tortilla taco bowl, ready to eat

TAKEAWAY SAVER

If you're like me, nothing can come between you and your food, especially when it's a gorgeous takeaway. So when your third aunt twice removed is calling for a catch-up as you arrive back home with the goods, the last thing you want to do is pick up. But you know you should, so here's how to keep your food warm.

Simply place your takeaway in the microwave and shut the door - it's insulated, so should retain the heat. Don't have a microwave? Minus 12 man points!

Piping-hot Kung Po Chicken

Microwave is open (close it!)

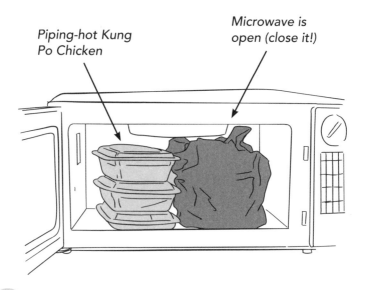

NO-TEARS ONIONS

Chopping an onion without breaking out in tears seems to many to be an impossible dream – unless you want to splash out on those goggles that make you look like a 1980s squash player. But there is another way.

Take your onion and put it in the freezer for 15 minutes. This method makes sure the eye-watering chemicals aren't released when you peel and cut it. Genius!

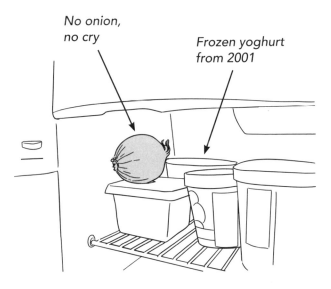

*No onion,
no cry*

*Frozen yoghurt
from 2001*

MULTI-SLICE DEVICE

Here's one for fans of the sweet and juicy cherry tomato (if you're not a fan you need to have a word with yourself – they're delicious). One thing that is annoying about them is that they're so damn small, so when it comes to slicing them you can be there all day. No longer!

Simply sandwich them between two small plates, applying just a little bit of pressure but leaving a gap all the way around. Next, take a knife longer than the diameter of the plates and slice between the plates, cutting the tomatoes all at once.

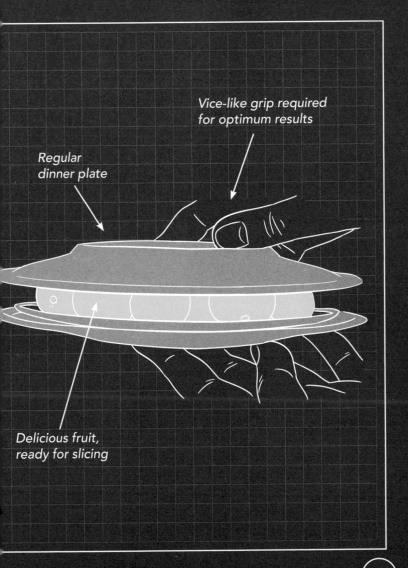

Vice-like grip required for optimum results

Regular dinner plate

Delicious fruit, ready for slicing

23

EASY-PEEL GARLIC

Peeling garlic is another fiddly job that can slow you down a bit in the kitchen. But nothing beats the fresh stuff, so here's how to get a head start.

For this hack you will need a cocktail shaker. (Again, if you don't have one, you should – every self-respecting man should be able to mix at least one cocktail. You can pick shakers up cheaply second-hand.) Throw in your garlic cloves and shake them vigorously for 20 seconds. You'll find that the skins have been shed, and those that are clinging on peel away easily.

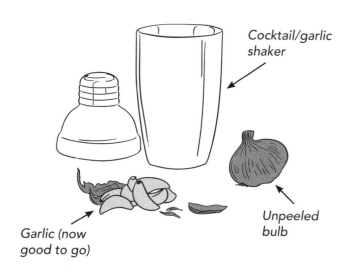

Cocktail/garlic shaker

Unpeeled bulb

Garlic (now good to go)

DRINKS HACKS

This chapter is mostly about that most joyful of beverages: alcohol. We're not saying that booze hacks are more important than, say, water hacks – but we're not *not* saying that either. Whether you need to open your bottle of wine with ease, require your drink to be cooled pronto or just want an ingenious way of never spilling your drink again, we have it covered.

THREE-PIN BOTTLE OPENER

Bottle openers are marvellous inventions, except when you lose them: then you're left cursing your way around the house trying to find something to open your beer with.

Next time you're on the rampage, consider the humble three-pin plug.

You know that water and electricity don't mix, but nowadays plugs (especially the ones that come with smartphones) are detachable. And if you have a smartphone, you're bound to have an extra plug doing nothing. Put it to use by turning it sideways and sliding the pins above and below the bottle cap. Apply pressure and *voilà*, your bottle is open.

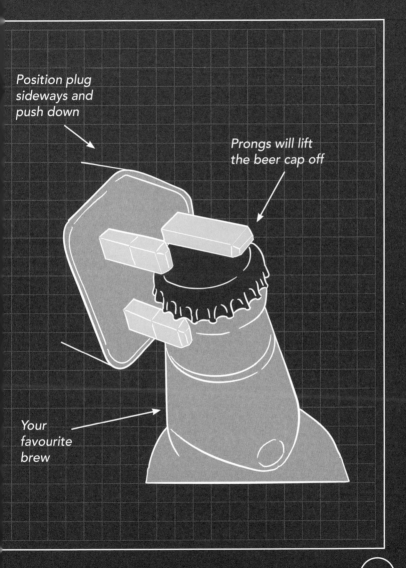

Position plug
sideways and
push down

Prongs will lift
the beer cap off

Your
favourite
brew

RIBBON RE-CORKER

If you've made the effort to buy decent wine for your dinner party you don't want to waste a drop – but sometimes you get overexcited and open a bottle that somehow doesn't get touched. Here's an elegant way of re-corking your precious vino. (This will only work if you haven't poured any wine out, though.)

Push the original cork all the way down into the bottle – it should be floating in the neck. Next, grab a length (8 inches/20 cm) of ribbon (1 inch/2 cm wide), loop it into a U shape and lower it into the bottle and underneath the bottom of the cork. Lift the cork up carefully with the ends of the ribbon while holding the bottom of the bottle. You now have a tight seal on your bottle, saving the wine to be drunk another day.

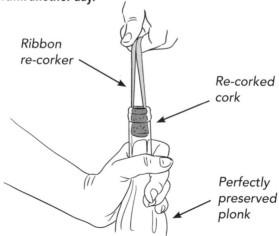

Ribbon
re-corker

Re-corked
cork

Perfectly
preserved
plonk

SALTY SUPER CHILLER

Whether you're having a party or lazing in the afternoon sun in the garden, a perfectly chilled batch of beers or soft drinks – or a bottle of champers if you're feeling saucy – is a must. Except when you've forgotten to chill them! In that case, you need this hack.

If you own an ice bucket, grab it; if not, use anything that is waterproof and bucket-like. Fill your receptacle with ice – so far, so familiar – but before you nestle your drinks into it shake a generous amount of salt over the ice, which will cause the ice to melt quicker. Seems wrong, but this will actually cool your drinks in a shorter amount of time.

Super-chilled beer

Beverage-specific container

BEER

BEER BOTTLE STACK

Drinkers have battled with this problem since the holy union of fridge and bottled beer was first realised – how to stack more than a few bottles in the fridge without taking up the whole fridge! Well, with this hack your prayers are answered.

Simply take a bulldog clip and attach it, facing upwards, to one of the rungs in your fridge shelf (this won't work for glass shelves, I'm afraid). You have now created a prop for the base layer of a beer bottle pyramid, meaning you can stack the precious suds up, rather than across. Genius!

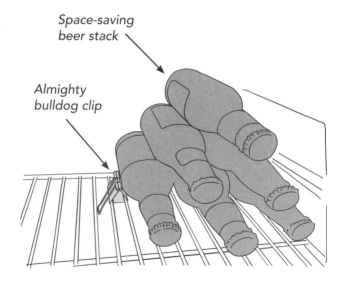

Space-saving beer stack

Almighty bulldog clip

COCONUT CURE

Maybe you're lucky and don't suffer too badly after a heavy night on the sauce – but if, like the rest of us, you wake up feeling like you've been run over by a bulldozer, this hack might just help.

Forget your fry-ups, energy drinks and hair of the dog – think coconuts. No, we're not talking about a holiday in the Bahamas, we're talking coconut water. It contains electrolytes – potassium, sodium, magnesium, phosphorus and calcium – which our bodies crave after a night of booze-fuelled indulgence. Drink it down and you'll be well on your way to recovery.

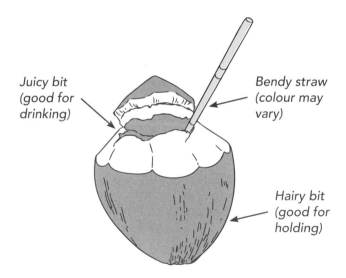

Juicy bit (good for drinking)

Bendy straw (colour may vary)

Hairy bit (good for holding)

HOW TO INTERACT WITH A BEER SNOB

For many, craft beer is the new wine, and even if you're not into it, any self-respecting man should at least know a little about it and its predecessor 'real ale' (if just to frustrate any beer snobs in your vicinity). Here are some key facts to help you hack your way through a beer conversation:

- Beer has four primary ingredients: water, hops, yeast and malt.

- British hops are earthy and floral, European hops are spicy and floral and American hops are bitter and can be citrusy.

- Craft beer began in America (Anchor Brewing in San Francisco is widely regarded as the oldest US craft brewer). It's usually carbonated, heavily chilled and not fermenting after it leaves the brewery, unlike real ale, which is never fizzy, only ever cool and continues to 'brew' in the cellar.

- Popular UK/US beer styles (going from light to dark colour) are: pale ale, IPA (India Pale Ale), amber ale, red ale, brown ale, porter, stout.

- IBU stands for International Bitterness Units.

Hop flower
(not a 'bud')

Various styles of beer

IPA   ESB   STOUT   MILD   PORTER

ALCOHOLICUBES

This hack is all about basic maths. Cider/wine + ice cubes (water) = cooler but diluted drink. Cider/wine + cider/wine cubes (additional alcohol) = cooler drink and more of it!

So instead of watering down your favourite tipple, dedicate a bottle to freezing in the ice cube tray, and next time you want to chill your booze you'll have the perfect way to do it. Just don't mix up your cider cubes and your wine cubes (unless you're into that sort of thing).

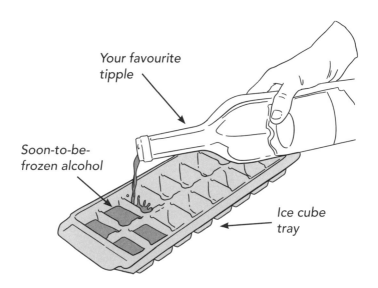

Your favourite tipple

Soon-to-be-frozen alcohol

Ice cube tray

VODKA ORANGE

This hack is guaranteed to get the party started (or turn an innocent picnic into a scene of boozed-up debauchery). Vodka and orange is a classic combo, but have you ever thought of combining vodka with an actual orange? Well, you can – and it tastes awesome.

You'll need a vodka miniature (trust me, it's enough) and a large orange. Cut a hole in the peel of the orange big enough for the neck of your miniature to pass through. Open your bottle and sit it upright on a flat surface, then stick your orange onto it, using the hole to wedge the bottle in. Carefully turn the bottle and orange upside down, so the bottle is allowed to release the vodka into the orange. Leave until all or most of the vodka has been sucked up and the result is a boozy orange that will definitely leave a sweet taste in your mouth.

Run-of-the-mill orange

Cheeky vodka injection

HACKS AROUND THE HOUSE

Every self-respecting man can hold his own when it comes to cleaning, tidying and organising around the house. No, it's not the most exciting of pastimes, but if you can keep a tidy wardrobe and a clean house you've got your sh*t together. This chapter gives you tips on everything from hanging your clothes correctly to making light work of essential household tasks.

MATTRESS DEEP CLEAN

You'll spend on average a third of your life asleep in bed so with this in mind it's probably a good idea to keep your mattress relatively clean. All you need is baking soda and a hoover. Sprinkle on a covering of baking soda, rub it in and leave it for at least an hour. Then plug your hoover in and suck up the soda, dust and dirt with it.

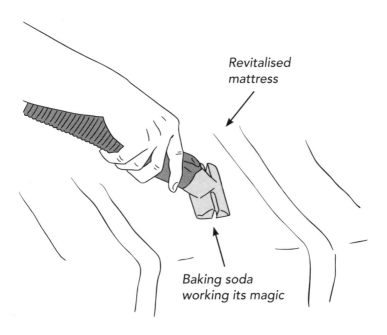

Revitalised mattress

Baking soda working its magic

DUST BUSTER

Those new blinds you had fitted look awesome, but the thick layer of dust that collects on them daily isn't a winner. However, cleaning them doesn't have to be as painful as you think.

Transform your BBQ tongs (old ones, preferably) into a handy blind-cleaning tool. Cover each side of the tongs with a duster and fasten with two elastic bands. Run the duster tongs over each slat in the blinds for easy cleaning.

Trusty tongs

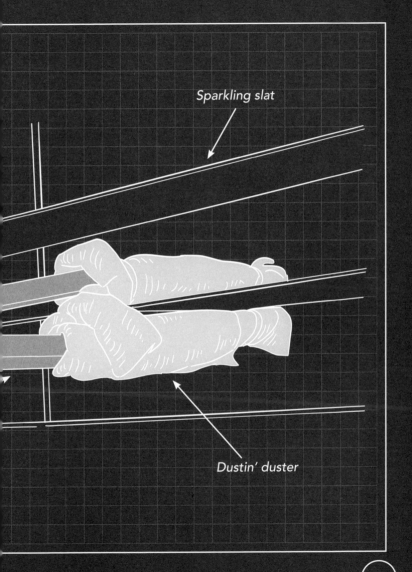

Sparkling slat

Dustin' duster

SOFA SANITISER

This hack will work wonders on your sofa (as long as the covering is synthetic material) if it's grimy from a party or it's simply seen too much backside and you want to refresh it.

Get yourself a bristle brush and rubbing alcohol. Saturate the area you want to clean with the alcohol – it will dry quickly in a darker colour to the rest of the material. Then take your scrubbing brush and, using circular motions, scrub away the marks. You'll never want to invite a guest over again.

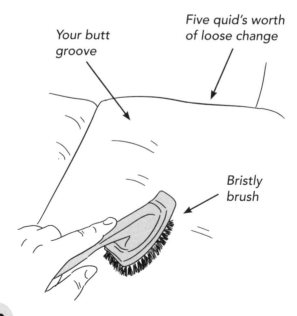

Your butt groove

Five quid's worth of loose change

Bristly brush

SPRAY LUBE
LOO CLEANER

Cleaning the loo is never going to be top of anyone's favourite things to do list, especially when the grime has built up. However, you can significantly increase the man factor of the chore by using none other than spray lube. No, it's not just for mechanical parts!

Spray a good amount around the toilet bowl for a couple of seconds. WD-40 will dissolve any grime lurking on the bowl. Scrub it with a brush for a minute or so for a glistening loo.

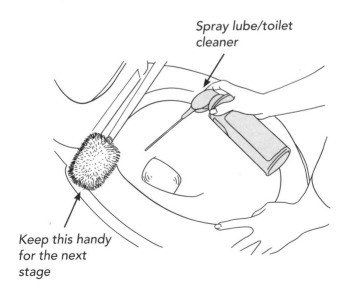

Spray lube/toilet cleaner

Keep this handy for the next stage

UNIVERSAL HOOVER NOZZLE

As dull and as boring as hoovering is, your life might be made a little bit easier and chores might be over quicker if all the extensions for the vacuum got into all the nooks and crannies around your home. So make yourself a universal nozzle that will make hoovering far simpler.

Use a cardboard toilet roll tube and slide it onto the hoover nozzle; being flexible, the cardboard can be bent to fit any area, however oddly shaped!

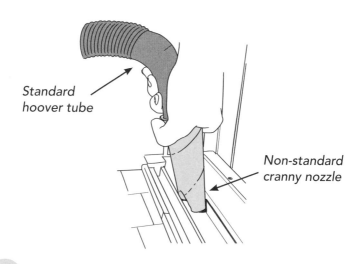

Standard
hoover tube

Non-standard
cranny nozzle

DISHWASHER DETOX

Believe it or not the thing that cleans your dishes may actually need cleaning itself from time to time. This hack will show you how.

All you need to do is put a half a pint of white vinegar on the top shelf and run the washer at the highest temperature. Then sprinkle the bottom shelf in baking soda and run again. Now you have yourself a properly performing dishwasher, which, instead of coating your dirty dishes with gunk, will leave them sparkling.

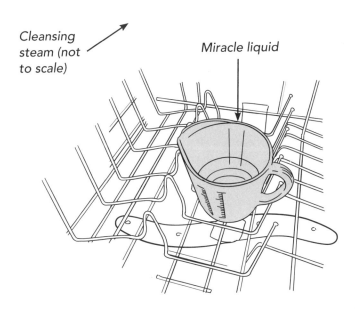

Cleansing steam (not to scale)

Miracle liquid

STOVETOP DEGREASER

If your stove top is greasier than a truck-stop cafe, you've got a problem. Firstly, why the hell aren't you cleaning it more?! Secondly, this hack will help restore it to its former glory. Adding yet more grease might not seem like such a great idea, but applying more oil will actually loosen those gunky splatters a lot more effectively than scrubbing alone.

Grab a paper towel, splash on a few drops of vegetable oil and wipe across the greased-up areas to clean it right off.

Don't attempt if these things are turned to 'On'

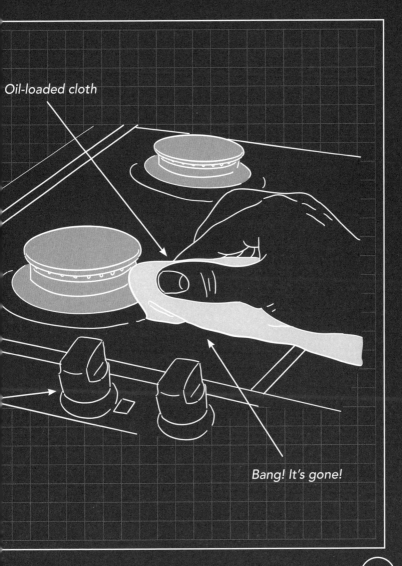

Oil-loaded cloth

Bang! It's gone!

IRONING OUT THE DENTS

This hack offers a simple solution for removing marks and dents on your wooden furniture and floors.

First, dampen the affected area with water and lay a paper towel over the top. Next, plug in the iron, let it heat up and proceed to apply pressure, in circular motions, across the paper. After a few minutes the heat and moisture will cause the wood to expand, leaving barely a trace!

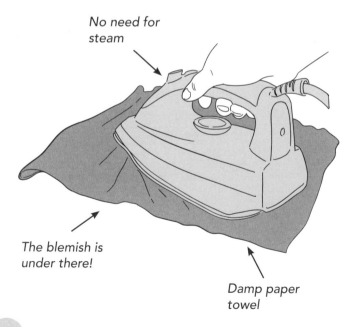

No need for steam

The blemish is under there!

Damp paper towel

CLOTHING HACKS

This chapter is all about clothing – not what to wear (you'll need to wait for the Fashion chapter for that), but neat ways of storing, folding and generally looking after it. If you're frustrated by ironing shirts, having too many pairs of socks or yearning to master the perfect way to fold a T-shirt, we've got you covered.

WINE RACK (FOR SHOES)

If you're a wine aficionado like me you'll have a healthy store of cardboard cases of the sort with dividers to keep the bottles in place. You might be doing your bit and recycling them, but you'd be doing wrong! Why throw them away when you can use them to organise your wardrobe?

If you have a mess of footwear at the bottom of your wardrobe, simply set one of your cases down on its side and use it as a makeshift shoe organiser. You're welcome.

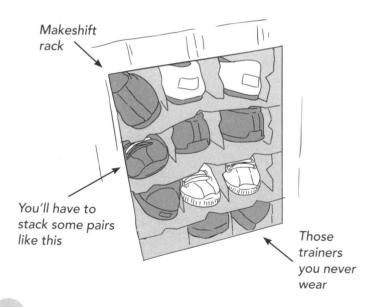

Makeshift rack

You'll have to stack some pairs like this

Those trainers you never wear

SOCK STORAGE SUCCESS

Picking the right socks for the right occasion is something every man needs to master. Not exactly rocket science – the hard part comes when you're left rifling through your over-full drawer trying to find the right socks! There has to be a better way of organising them, and there is.

Take your socks and lay them down in a plus shape – the first sock vertically, the second horizontally. Fold the ankle end of the vertical sock over the top of the horizontal one, followed by the toe end. Then tuck the ankle and toe end of the horizontal sock underneath the folds of the vertical one. You are left with a neat sock packet that you can stand up in your drawer, keeping your socks in place and making them more visible.

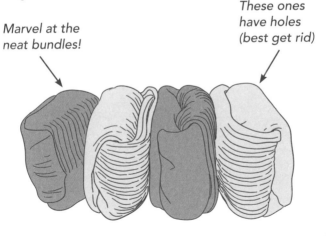

Marvel at the neat bundles!

These ones have holes (best get rid)

JUMPER HANGER

For the jumper-loving man who is not a fan of a stretched neck or unsightly lumps in the shoulders of his knitwear, this hack, using a simple coat-hanger, has got you covered.

To begin, fold your jumper in half lengthways, with the sleeves lined up and resting to one side (see diagram 1). Lay your coat-hanger upside down at an angle on top of the jumper, with the hook just peeking over the armpit (see diagram 2). Fold the bottom hem up to the collar and wrap the sleeves over too (see diagram 3). Stow your perfectly folded jumper in your wardrobe.

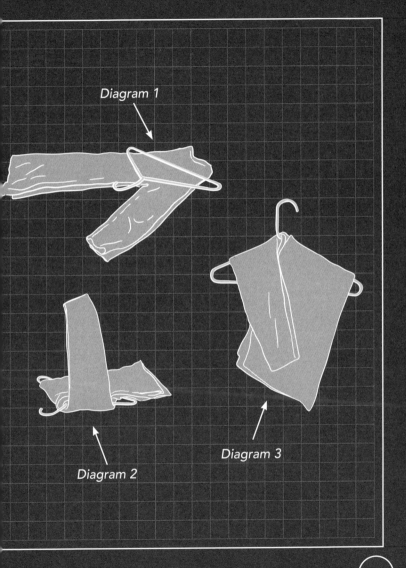

Diagram 1

Diagram 2

Diagram 3

BELT COLLAR SAVER

Don't you just hate it when you've painstakingly ironed every little crease out of your shirt, only for it to be transformed into a squashed-up mess after it's been in your bag or case for no more than 5 minutes? How can you impress at an interview/wedding/multi-million-pound merger when your collar looks like it's been chewed on by a dog or a small child?

Folding your shirt correctly can help overall, but using this no-brainer hack will seal the deal. Simply loop your belt inside the upstanding collar of your shirt to ensure it stays in shape while being transported.

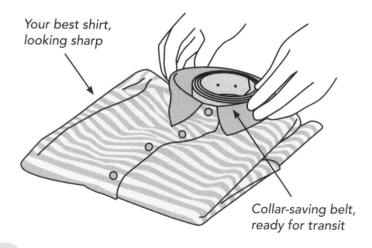

Your best shirt, looking sharp

Collar-saving belt, ready for transit

BLOW AWAY THE WRINKLES

This is a quick cheat for the times when you can't be bothered to dig out the ironing board and the iron (or, like many people nowadays, if you don't own these things!). That said, you do need a hairdryer – if you don't have one yourself, hopefully you can borrow one from another member of the household.

To de-wrinkle a piece of clothing simply dampen the affected area(s) with water, set the hairdryer on a low heat and blow-dry until the creases disappear.

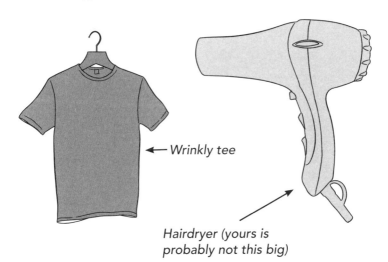

← *Wrinkly tee*

Hairdryer (yours is probably not this big)

EASY-IRON SHIRT

If you're planning on wearing a shirt to look your best, there's no substitute for breaking out the iron and pressing it properly. This hack will make the job that bit easier.

It's really awkward to get in between the buttons on the front of your shirt with an iron – that is, unless you turn your shirt over and iron the buttons from the back. The iron can still do its job without getting caught up. Easy!

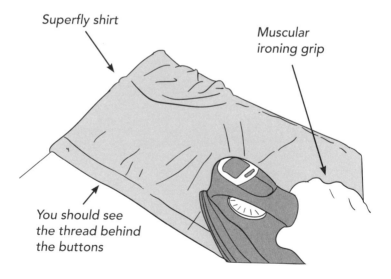

Superfly shirt

Muscular ironing grip

You should see the thread behind the buttons

WHITER FOR LONGER

A white dress shirt should be a staple in every man's wardrobe. But the problem with white clothes is that even the lightest mark shows up. When it comes to discolouring around the collar and armpits, this hack has got you covered.

Sprinkle talcum powder onto these areas before you iron. The powder will form a barrier between the clothing and the oils from your skin, making sure that no matter what the day throws at you, your shirt won't bear the evidence.

Yet another superfly shirt

Talc (it says so on the bottle)

TALC

TWO-SECOND T-SHIRT FOLD

OK, so if it's your first time doing this it will take you more than 2 seconds, but it's fast and it will save you time and effort when you're packing. Lay your shirt flat and in your mind's eye draw a horizontal line across the middle of your T-shirt. Then imagine a line going from the shoulder furthest away from you vertically to the bottom of the shirt. Pinch where the lines intersect (see point A), and with the other hand pick up the shoulder (see point B). Bring the shoulder down to the bottom edge (point C), and pick up. Holding all the points, lift the T-shirt up, pulling the shoulder (now attached to point C), back up. Lower the shirt back down to the surface, while tucking the sleeve underneath to make a neat rectangle.

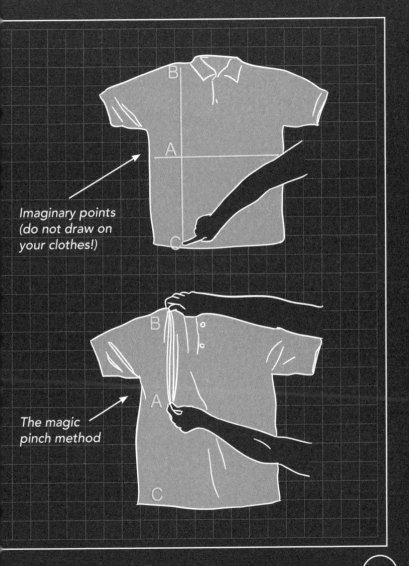

Imaginary points (do not draw on your clothes!)

The magic pinch method

57

NO-WAX SLACKS

OK, so perhaps this is more of a 'once in a blue moon' hack, but when that day/night does come around you'll be grateful we told you what to do! In the event of getting wax on your trousers (maybe you've been to a Halloween party or a Jane Austen convention), here's what you should do.

Take a plain piece of paper, roughly A4 size, and place it over the dry wax. Next, run a hot iron over the paper a few times and the wax on your clothes will transfer onto the piece of paper, almost like magic!

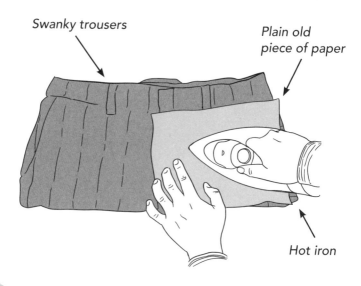

Swanky trousers

Plain old piece of paper

Hot iron

SPORTS HACKS

If you like playing sports, chances are a few of the awesome tricks in this chapter will raise your game. If you're not such a fan, these hacks will help you look like a pro without all the effort. Sadly, there are no hacks to help you watch sports, but we're pretty sure you can handle that yourself.

TOASTY TEE-OFF

Hitting a drive straight down the fairway is challenging at the best of times, even if you do have the latest club-head technology at your disposal. Millions have been spent on improving the club, but what about the ball?

Studies have shown that a warm ball carries further than a cold one. So, slip your go-to ball into your pocket while you make your way down to the course, and by the time you're ready to tee off it'll be primed for smashing.

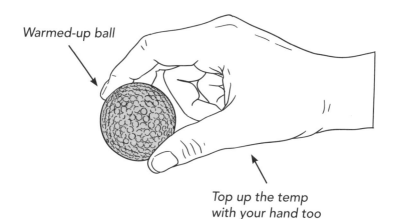

Warmed-up ball

Top up the temp
with your hand too

PUTT-RITE

Like Happy Gilmore, many golfers struggle with their short game. In real life you won't have Carl Weathers to coach you on the green, so get smart with this no-frills ball-alignment hack.

To add your own alignment marks to your balls, simply take the plastic ring from underneath the cap of a flask-style bottle of soft drink (the brand that combines 'alliGATOR' and 'lemonADE' is perfect for this) and slot it around your ball. Draw your lines and you now have an easy way to line up your putts.

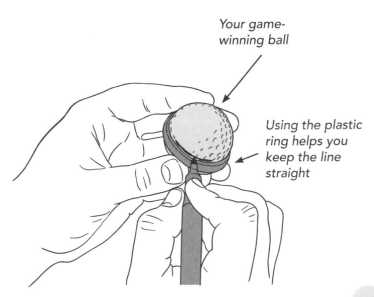

Your game-winning ball

Using the plastic ring helps you keep the line straight

GLOVELESS GRIP

Some might consider wearing a glove while golfing as essential, but here's a hack for those who prefer to play *au naturel*.

To keep your grip sticky, spray your palms with deodorant. This will create a bit of sweet-smelling friction between your hands and the club, ensuring every stroke is a success.

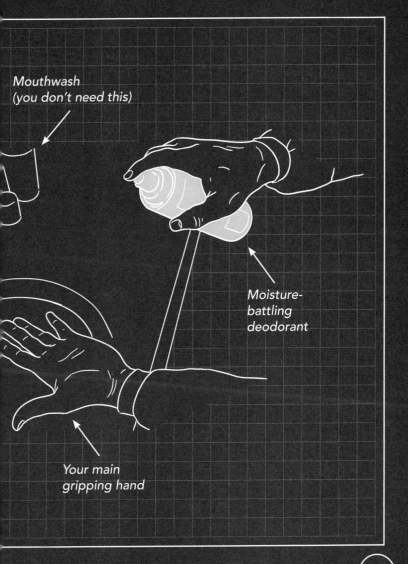

Mouthwash
(you don't need this)

Moisture-battling
deodorant

Your main
gripping hand

LUCKY HAT WASH

Whether your hat really is lucky, you wear it to look good or it's just something to keep the sun off your bald spot, washing the thing is likely to be a challenge. If, like many of the pros, you favour the classic peaked cap, there's a simple way of getting it clean without it coming out like it's been chewed by the dog.

Place it in the dishwasher (minus detergent and dirty dishes) and it will re-emerge looking as good as the day you bought it.

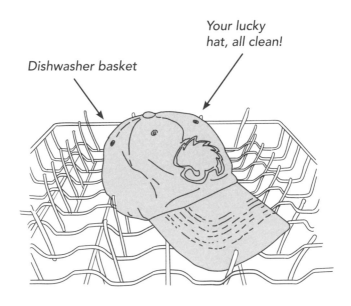

Your lucky hat, all clean!

Dishwasher basket

CLUB PROP

Putting your golf clubs down onto grass (damp or otherwise) is a school-boy error, but when you're focussing hard it's easy for your mind to slip. So here's how to avoid it.

Use a tee or divot-repair tool stuck into the ground to prop the end of your club up. Just don't be a dummy and trip over it!

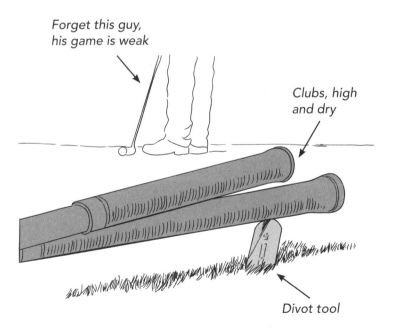

Forget this guy, his game is weak

Clubs, high and dry

Divot tool

NEW BOOT BREAK-IN

Instead of having a few off games while you're wearing in your brand new boots (football, rugby, or whatever sport you're into) wear them in the quick way with hot water. If they're real leather boots, coat them with dubbin or leather care treatment first to prevent cracks.

Put on your game socks, followed by your boots. Next, immerse both feet into a bowl of hot (not boiling) water. Wiggle your toes and move your feet to stretch the boots out a bit. After the boot material has loosened, take the boots off and stuff them with newspaper so they keep their shape. Tie the laces tight and wait for them to dry on the washing line for around 8-10 hours.

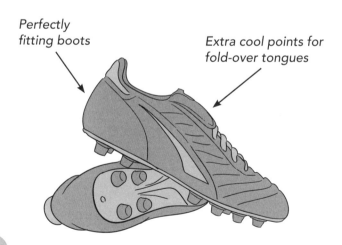

Perfectly fitting boots

Extra cool points for fold-over tongues

BLISTER BUSTER

Blisters are one of the least impressive ailments you can get, but boy oh boy do they smart! Anything that stops you running properly in a match is a nightmare, but you can put an end to that bad dream.

Before you put your boots on, just swipe or spray on some anti-perspirant anywhere you think is rubbing. The deodorant reduces sweating and will act as a barrier that protects your feet from friction.

Blister-free foot

Deodorant (don't buy expensive stuff, it's for your feet!)

FISH ODOUR ELIMINATOR

If you love the tranquillity of the outdoors combined with the peacefulness of a steady-flowing river or still lake, fishing is the pastime for you. But if you actually expect to catch something, you'd better be ready to enjoy squirming livebait and slimy, stinky fish too. With this hack your days of smelling like the Creature from the Black Lagoon will soon be gone.

To de-stink your hands, wash them as you normally would and then press and run your hands over a stainless steel surface – the sink, some cutlery, a bowl. A chemical reaction takes place that removes the odour-causing molecules from the skin.

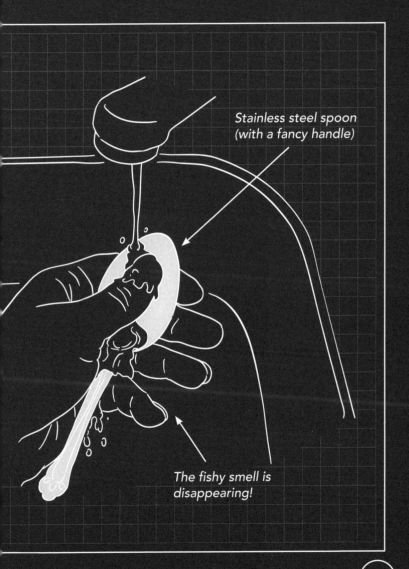

Stainless steel spoon (with a fancy handle)

The fishy smell is disappearing!

ANTI-TANGLE SPOOL

Tangled line is the bane of every fisherman's life. It's bad enough when the fish aren't biting, but if you've spent 30 minutes getting your tackle ready only for it to tangle on the first cast, you will be ranting.

A spool with new line will often tangle. To help prevent this, take the lot and run it underneath the hot tap for 2 to 3 minutes. The heat will help the line relax onto the spool and ensure your casts are as smooth as a carp's underbelly.

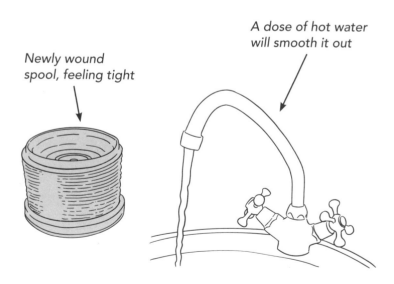

Newly wound spool, feeling tight

A dose of hot water will smooth it out

ALL HOOKED UP

Man vs fish is an age-old battle that has been played out for centuries on lakes, rivers and seas across the globe. As if a lack of interest on the end of a fisherman's line wasn't enough to contend with, one thing that every angler has to overcome is the fiddliness of the tackle, which inevitably comes in finger-flummoxing packaging. None more so than hooks, which is why this hack is a winner.

Instead of blowing a fuse trying to pinch a new hook out of its tiny packet, and getting spiked in the process, take an old wine cork and push your hooks into one end. This way, they are fully sheathed and wholly accessible for the next time you face off against **Old Green Gills**.

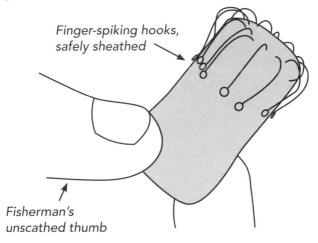

Finger-spiking hooks, safely sheathed

Fisherman's unscathed thumb

THE PERFECT SPOT

Finding the best fishing spot can seem like an impossible task. Is it luck? Is it some ancient wisdom that you only acquire after 50 years and an excess of ear hair? Of course not - it's science.

Any fisherman worth his waders knows that fish like to gather near a natural shelf. So you just need to find an area where the shallows drop away to deeper water (you can use a plumb bob for this) and focus your efforts there.

They're over here!

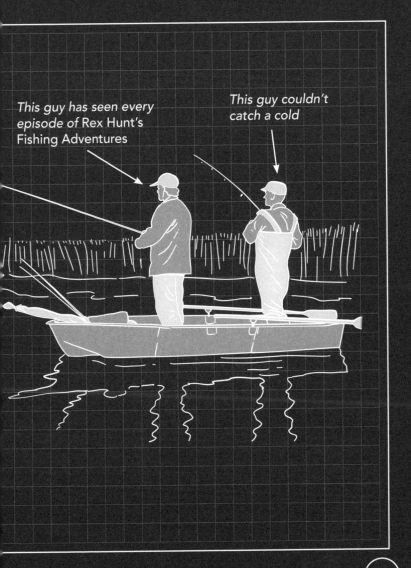

CHAFING PREVENTION

There are certain sports that are more irritating than others. No, I'm not talking about extreme ironing, I'm talking about chafing. Running, cycling and anything that involves extended periods of fast(ish) movement causes friction at various contact points, which means irritation.

Combat this by greasing up with petroleum jelly (the cheaper alternative to sports-specific stuff). Nipples, inner thighs, groin – all of these soft spots can be helped with a dab of embrocation.

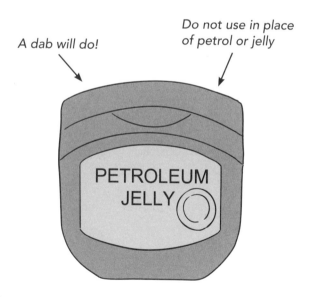

A dab will do!

Do not use in place of petrol or jelly

PETROLEUM JELLY

FREE YOUR POCKETS

When you're slipping out for a run you want to ensure you're not carrying anything you don't absolutely need. As such, some running gear is designed without pockets – great for keeping it minimal on your run, bad for taking essentials like keys with you. This hack gives you a nifty way of keeping your house key safe when you're running light.

It's a simple matter of lacing it up into your running shoe – go at least two holes down and be sure to tuck the free end of the key in to stop it moving while you're running.

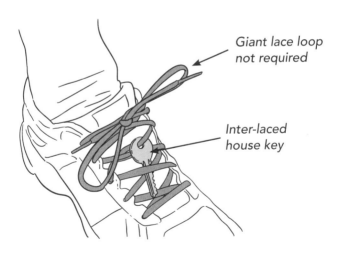

Giant lace loop
not required

Inter-laced
house key

BEGINNER RUNNING PLAN

You might have considered starting running and thought, 'How hard can it be? It's running! Surely you just start running!' Well, you'd be wrong. That is, there is a more advisable way to break yourself in to this awesome sport. Follow this daily plan and you'll be pounding the pavement like a champ in no time:

> Week 1: Run for 2 minutes, walk for 3 minutes, repeat six times.
> Week 2: Run for 3 minutes, walk for 3, repeat five times.
> Week 3: Run for 5 minutes, walk for 2, repeat four times.
> Week 4: Run 7 minutes, walk for 3, repeat three times.
> Week 5: Run 8 minutes, walk 2, repeat three times.
> Week 6: Run 9 minutes, walk 1 minute, repeat three times.
> Week 7: Run 30 minutes.

BIKE HACKS

Bicycles are one of the most efficient and convenient modes of transport ever invented. Yes, many people leave them behind at the age of 12, but those who choose to cycle as an adult quickly realise how cool it is. You don't need to squash yourself into tight, stretchy clothes (unless you want to) – there are endless practical ways to use a bike, and all of them are fun. These hacks will help you on your way.

COMMANDO RIDING

Those of you who are new to the world of cycling in Lycra might find that your nether regions can quickly get uncomfortable – not because of a rock-hard saddle (although that doesn't help), but because you've forgotten to lose your undercrackers.

Yes, as weird as it sounds, cycling shorts are designed to be worn directly next to the skin – no pants required. Even cycling-specific underwear ultimately gets in the way if you're wearing stretchy clothes to begin with. So if you're a newbie, do yourself a favour and lose the kecks to avoid groin-related discomfort.

Bunching will occur around here

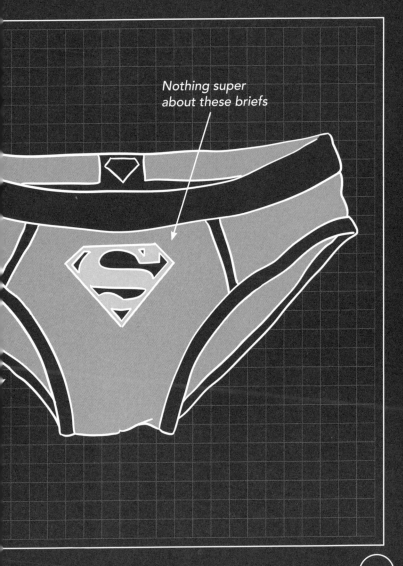

Nothing super about these briefs

GO THE EXTRA MILE

Sport-specific equipment is expensive. Often you get what you pay for, but when you do you want to get as much use out of it as possible. So don't be a dummy when it comes to buying new bicycle tyres. Yes, it makes sense to buy two at once – there are two wheels after all! – but if you look closely you'll see the back tyre wears a lot more quickly than the front.

So, before you take the plunge and buy new ones, switch the more-worn back tyre to the front, and the front to the back. Extra miles for your tyres, extra saving time for you.

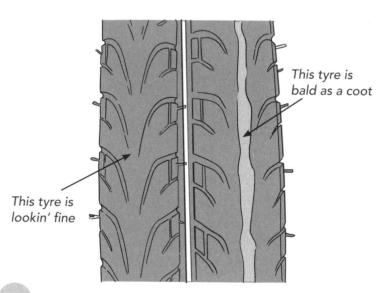

This tyre is bald as a coot

This tyre is lookin' fine

WET-WEATHER WHEELS

Braving the elements is part and parcel of cycling if you choose to do it on a regular basis. Rain is one of the least enjoyable conditions when you're out on your bike, but as well as taking precautions to keep yourself safe and dry you should also consider your bike - specifically, your wheels.

Lowering your tyre pressure by 5–10 psi will improve your grip on wet roads. To do this more or less exactly you'll need a pump with a pressure gauge. If you don't have one, just let a small amount of air out the old-fashioned way.

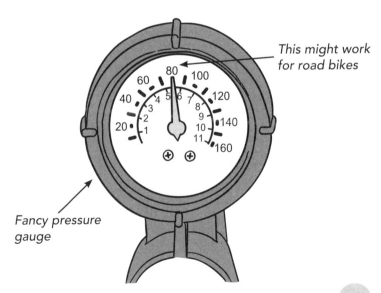

This might work for road bikes

Fancy pressure gauge

HEAVY METAL CYCLING

If you're at a point with your cycling where you've been riding for long enough to want to upgrade to a shiny new (most likely lighter) bike, you might well be the kind of rider who's in it for the fitness rather than the pure enjoyment. If so, and you're about to make that big purchase, don't automatically assume your old bike will now be defunct.

Older (most likely heavier) bikes are the perfect fitness training tool – the more load you're pulling the fitter you'll be. So save that new bike for race day, and do your training on your old clunker. And remember – you can never have too many bikes!

Feeling the need for speed

Race-day bike

MOUNTAIN BIKE PUNCTURE PREP

There are dozens of ways to carry gear on a bike – in jersey pockets, in saddle bags and so on – but none of those solutions are as nifty as this one. If you've been riding for a while you should already be carrying puncture repair materials, but here's a cool way of including an extra inner tube on your rides (that is, if you ride a fandangled mountain bike with more than two triangles in the frame).

Attach your additional inner tube to the inside of your seat tube triangle with electrical tape for a fit-and-forget back-up inner tube.

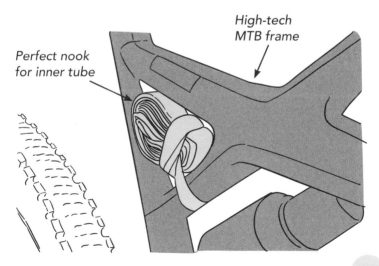

High-tech MTB frame

Perfect nook for inner tube

CHAIN STAY PROTECTOR

If you've been cycling long enough you will have almost certainly collected a number of 'dead' inner tubes: that is, inner tubes you have repaired several times and simply can't be bothered to persevere with any longer. But you don't need to leave them hanging around in your garage – you can use at least one as a chain stay protector.

Cut the spent inner tube into an inch-wide strip and tightly wrap it around the chain stay, tucking the loose ends in. Fasten with two cable ties, one at each end, and you're done!

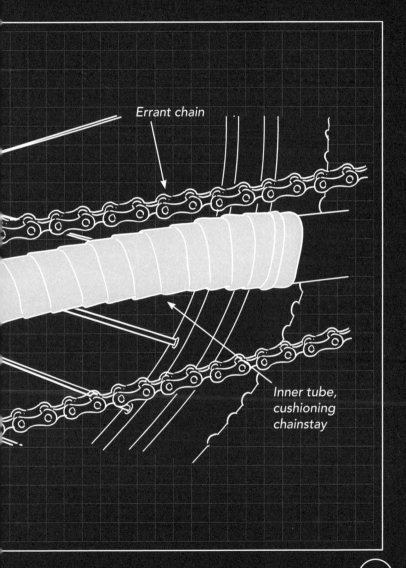

Errant chain

Inner tube,
cushioning
chainstay

EASY-REACH RIDE FUEL

The more you ride, the more you want to ride, and often this means getting more serious about the distances you cover. You might feel like you can ride forever – it's just pedalling after all – but long-distance riding requires you to consider all sorts of factors, and food is one of them. Enter energy gels. Most riders store them in a jersey pocket, but it's always awkward to reach back there while on your bike. So here's another way.

Tape your gel sachets (individually) to your top tube for easier access. Be sure to secure the sachet above the tear perforation, so you can remove and open it all in one quick motion.

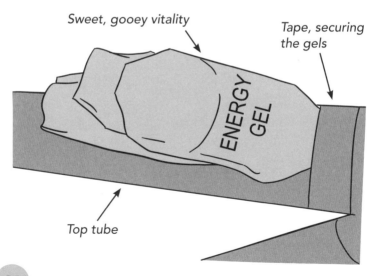

Sweet, gooey vitality

Tape, securing the gels

ENERGY GEL

Top tube

NO-FLAP HYDRATION PACK

Hydration packs (or 'bladders') for cycling are a godsend when you're looking to cover major distances. There's no awkward reaching to grab your bidon or fiddling to put it back in – you just angle the 'feed' tube into your mouth and take a refreshing glug. The problem is, on some packs the tube has been designed to flap freely, meaning that it can end up further away from your mouth than you'd like; not, however, when you use this simple hack.

Clamp your tube in place, onto your strap and thus closer to your mouth, with a humble bulldog clip. No more gurning to catch the nozzle!

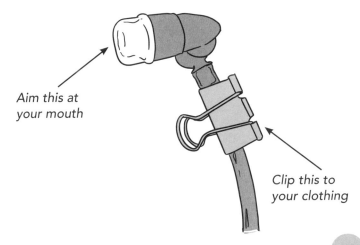

Aim this at your mouth

Clip this to your clothing

MAKESHIFT BIKE LIGHT

Being seen when riding at night is imperative. Nowadays it's easy – you can buy a host of hi-vis, reflective clothing and lights that can be seen from space (no, not really). When it comes to lights, however, prices can get a little steep. If you're a dedicated commuter, shelling out will totally be worth it, but if you're a more casual rider you might want to consider this budget option.

Double up the use of your pocket torch by making it into a makeshift front light for cycling. Take an old inner tube and cut it to the length of your torch. Next, carve out two holes an inch away from each end of the tube, and just a little bit smaller than the circumference of your torch. Wrap the tube under your handlebar and slide the torch through the holes. *Voilà*! Your makeshift light is good to go.

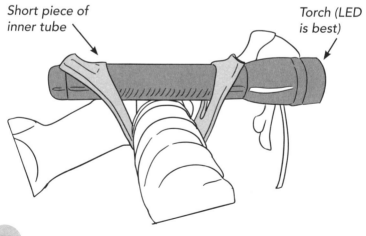

Short piece of inner tube

Torch (LED is best)

HANDLEBAR STOPPER

Whichever style of bike you ride, you're bound to have some kind of bung at the end of your bars. For road bikes this is mostly to hold your grip tape in place, while for others it's mostly to make the bar end less sharp and prone to damage. In all cases, the damn things are likely to fall out and get lost at some point!

When this happens, you'll need a replacement. Instead of traipsing down to your local bike shop, why not slip into your kitchen instead (or wine cellar, if you're so blessed) and break open a bottle or two of wine. After the arduous task of drinking your way through two bottles (not all at once!), you'll have yourself a pair of artisanal bar bungs in the form of your wine corks.

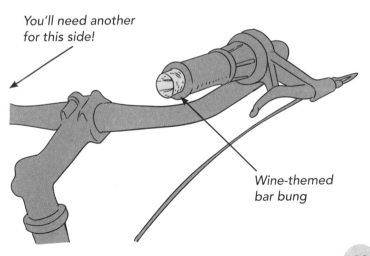

You'll need another for this side!

Wine-themed bar bung

BIKE CHAIN BRUSH-UP

Gadgets that make messy jobs like cleaning and lubing your bike easier are great, but they also come at a cost. Next time you're giving your bike chain some attention (degreasing or lubing), check out this budget hack.

Two toothbrushes taped together (old ones if you have them, cheap new ones if you don't) makes for a great chain lubing device (to spread oil evenly and brush away rust), as well as a degreasing device (though you will use more degreaser with this method). Simply hold the toothbrushes steady while you turn the pedals and steadily feed your chain through the two brush heads.

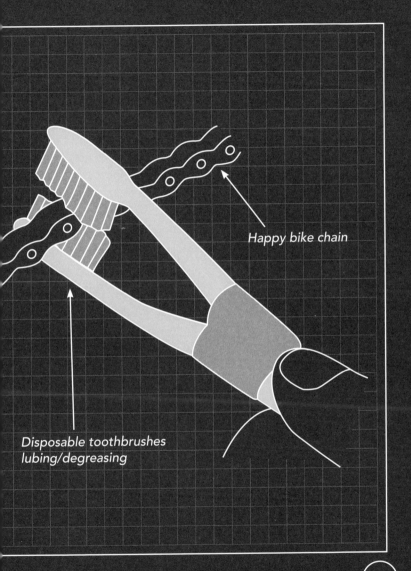

Happy bike chain

Disposable toothbrushes lubing/degreasing

CHAMOIS CARRY

Having all the gear for cycling can become an obsession. There's a product for every possible scenario and for the most part these are justified. There's lots to consider when you're cycle touring, including ensuring your 'saddle area' is catered for. Chamois cream is what you need, and this hack will make it easier to pack and carry just the right amount while on the move.

An old contact lens case is the perfect vessel to hold just enough chamois cream for a couple of top-ups should you need them on your ride. If you have 20/20 vision, the small plastic pots you can buy for airline travel are also very useful.

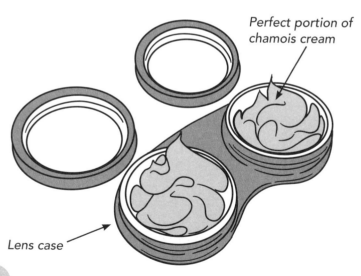

Perfect portion of chamois cream

Lens case

VEHICLE HACKS

For many men, their vehicle is their pride and joy – and understandably, as they are so ridiculously expensive to buy and run! Combine this with the fact that modern cars and bikes have become so inaccessible that you can't even change a headlight bulb without taking it to an authorised garage and you can see you need all the help you can get. Thankfully, this chapter is full of such help, both hi-tech and bog-standard.

DE-MISTING MEASURE

A misted visor in cold-weather conditions is as annoying as it gets for a motorbike rider. It's bad enough having to contend with the cold, but not being able to see properly is treacherous. Nowadays helmet and visor technology has advanced to help eliminate fogging – that is, if you can afford it.

For those who can't, here's a cheap and cheerful anti-fog measure. Grab a microfibre cloth, add to it a few drops of washing-up liquid and rub over the inside of your visor. Leave to dry for 20 minutes and buff away the white marks to finish.

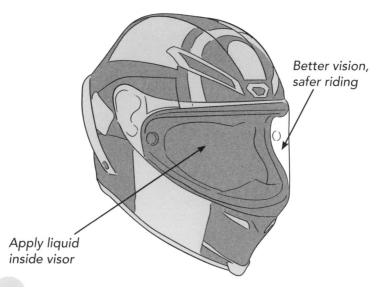

Better vision, safer riding

Apply liquid inside visor

THE CAN STAND

This hack is more for those who ride hogs as opposed to hairdryers. If you own a heavy-duty machine and you pull in for a pit stop on soft ground, such as a verge or maybe even a sedate village green, you'll have to watch where you're putting your kickstand. Soft ground + heavy bike with weight focussed on a small area = toppled ride. Here's how to prevent it.

Reach into your saddlebag (or pop into that quaint post office on the corner) for a can of soft drink. Empty its contents – down your gullet, preferably – and crush the can flat to form a solid spot for your stand to stand on.

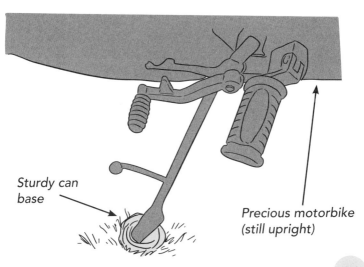

Sturdy can base

Precious motorbike (still upright)

QUICK GUIDE TO JUMP-STARTING

Here's a trick every vehicle owner should know how to execute (and one of the few things you don't need the official garage mechanic to do). When your battery is flat and you're stuck, the temptation is to call out the repair guy, but if you're in a residential area it could well be quicker to ask a kindly stranger to give you a jump-start. For those who know, here's a reminder. For those who don't – you're welcome. (Plus, now you know you can repay the favour and help someone else out.)

- Red on dead positive

- Red on donor positive

- Black on donor negative

- Black on something metal (such as the bonnet)

- Start the donor, then start the dead and remove leads in 4, 3, 2, 1.

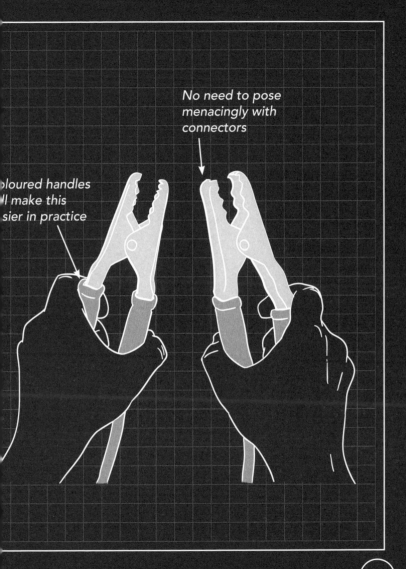

No need to pose
menacingly with
connectors

loured handles
ll make this
sier in practice

TWENTY-PENCE TREAD CHECK

Do any of us really know how deep the tread of our tyres is supposed to be? It is either new or completely and utterly bald; the in-between is a mystery to most. Here's a quick way to solve it using a twenty-pence piece.

Place the coin firmly into the main tread, and check if you can see any of the outer band (where the writing is) peeking above the tread. Do this across the tread to get a clear picture. If you see a lot of band, it's time to visit the garage.

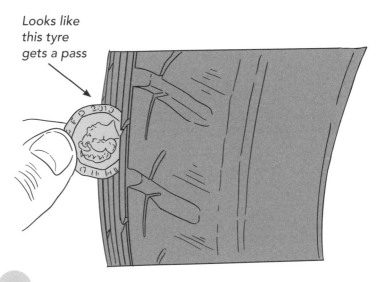

Looks like this tyre gets a pass

CUP HOLDER ORGANISER

Remember when cup holders in cars were a radical new invention? No, I don't either. Lots of cars have them now, but chances are you don't use them for holding drinks. Chances are you use them for storing tat - loose change, batteries, crisp wrappers, chewing gum. All of which becomes impossible to fish out again, because the holders are so narrow and, you know, made for cups. But here's a way of making them function better.

Line the bottom of your cup holders with cupcake cases. That way, you can grab the edge of the case and easily lift out your tiny bits of junk all at once.

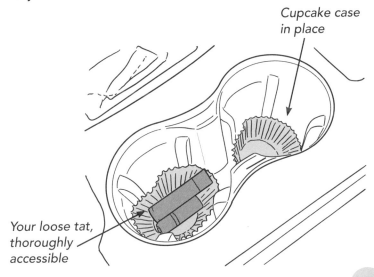

Cupcake case
in place

Your loose tat,
thoroughly
accessible

QUICK CAR COOLER

Getting into a hot car is like getting into a giant oven, albeit a very plush one. If you're faced with this disagreeable scenario, don't bother turning the air con on, use this nifty trick instead.

Roll one window in the car all the way down, and then open and close the door on the other side five or six times. Hot air will be forced out and your car will cool down instantly!

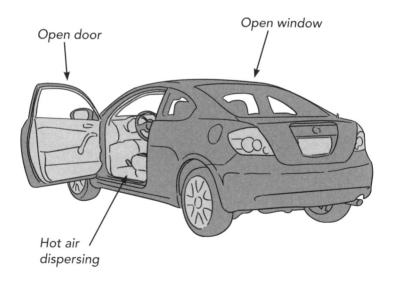

Open door

Open window

Hot air
dispersing

DRY-ICE DENT REMOVER

If you're the kind of car owner that doesn't care much about how your motor looks, this one isn't for you. If, however, you take pride in your car but can't bear the thought of extortionate bodywork costs, listen up. If you're unlucky enough to get a small to medium-sized ding in your car, remember to add dry ice onto your shopping list. (You can find it for little cost all over the internet.)

All you need to do is put on gloves (essential – otherwise the cold will burn your skin) and press the dry ice onto the dent for a few seconds. The low temp will cause the metal body to contract and the dent to pop out. Repeat this until the dent has disappeared.

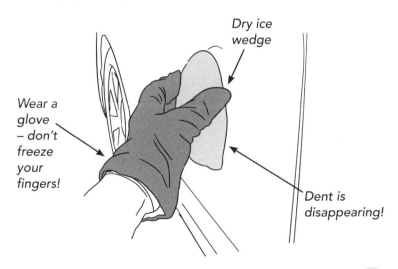

Dry ice wedge

Wear a glove – don't freeze your fingers!

Dent is disappearing!

FEATHERWEIGHT CAR KEYS

This one won't count if you have a fancy keyless car, but for those of us who are still using keys like Neanderthals, here's one way of extending the life of your ignition.

Unload your keyring to include only your car key(s). If you carry a bunch around like a Victorian jail keeper, the weight of your keys when inside the ignition could actually be causing undue wear and tear to the ignition. So keep it simple and separate the rest!

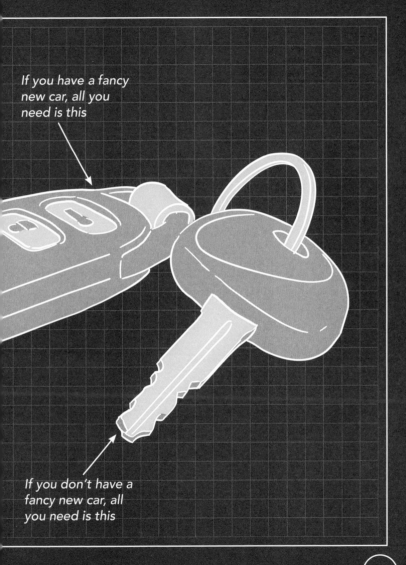

If you have a fancy new car, all you need is this

If you don't have a fancy new car, all you need is this

PARKING PINPOINTER

We've all been there. Parked in an obscenely large car park and returned to what you thought was the right spot, only you can't see your beloved motor. How can you lose something as big as a car? Well, you can, and you will. Unless you use this trick.

Before walking away from your car, get your phone out and select maps. Pin and save your location on your smartphone. Simple.

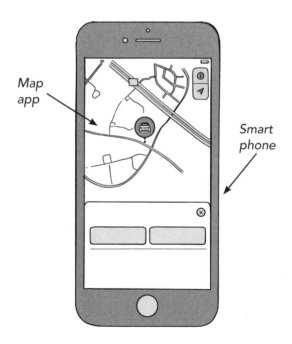

Map app

Smart phone

SEAT SETTING MARKER

It can take a while for you to find the perfect position for your driving seat, but when you do it's glorious. So when you find, after a service, it's been tampered with, you're going to be annoyed. That is, unless you use this hack.

Simply cut two thin strips of hard-wearing sticky tape, place one on the trim closest to your seat and the other directly in line with it on the trim of the seat itself. That way, if somebody messes with the position, you have two markers you can line up to get the perfect position back again.

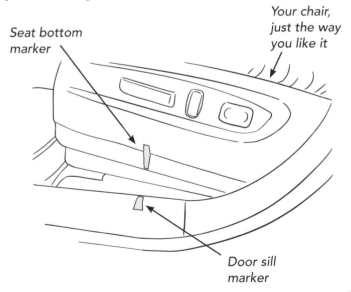

Seat bottom marker

Your chair, just the way you like it

Door sill marker

WINDSCREEN WIZARD

If you believe those dramatic commercials, a chip in your windscreen could develop into a devastating crack in the blink of an eye. That may be exaggerating slightly, but the truth is a chip is bad news. If you're strapped for cash, try this hack to tide you over until you can get it looked at.

Simply paint a thin layer of clear nail polish onto the chip – inside and out – to reinforce it and give you some peace of mind. You don't have any nail varnish, you say? What's wrong with you – it's the twenty-first century, man! (It can be picked up cheaply from any pharmacy.)

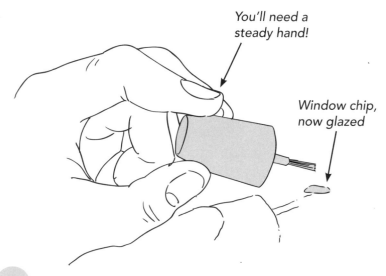

You'll need a
steady hand!

Window chip,
now glazed

RUBBER-BAND PHONE MOUNT

Smartphones are amazing gadgets and they can even be useful while driving – that is, if you're using them hands-free*. You might want to listen to some tunes or use the map function to find your way around. That's all well and good, but how can you make it easier? Here's how.

Take a rubber band and thread it through the slats in your fan/air con outlet so that you have two loops sticking out, top and bottom. Then just slide your phone under the loops to create a DIY phone holder.

* You should never, under any circumstances, use your phone while driving unless it is hands-free. It's illegal and dangerous.

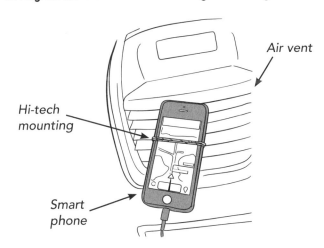

Air vent

Hi-tech mounting

Smart phone

HI-VIS DOORS

Despite cars nowadays being packed full of complex, advanced technology, there are some things that don't need a multi-million pound upgrade. Reflectors are such things. Cars still have them, but not in all places. So what, you say. Well, as the saying goes, on the road it's what the other idiots are doing that you need to look out for. By increasing the visibility of your doors at night, you could well avoid a nasty door-opening mishap.

Just stick some reflective tape on the inside ends of your doors and you will be safe and be seen.

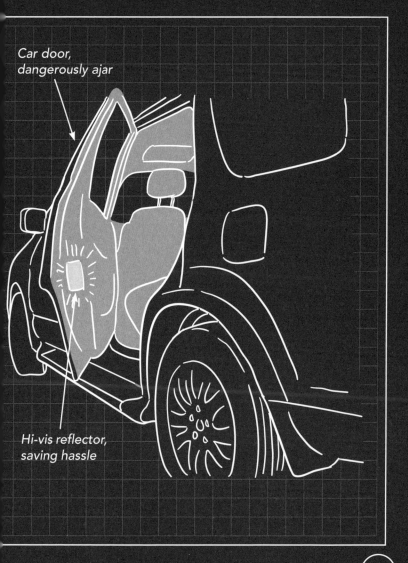

Car door,
dangerously ajar

Hi-vis reflector,
saving hassle

SCRATCH SEALER

Another chance to break out the nail varnish! This time it's for sealing scratches. If you're unlucky enough to get a scratch that's crept down to the bare metal you'll need to cover it quickly to prevent rust. And, yes, you've guessed it – you can use nail varnish.

Spread a thin layer onto the affected area to seal the scratch until you can get it looked at.

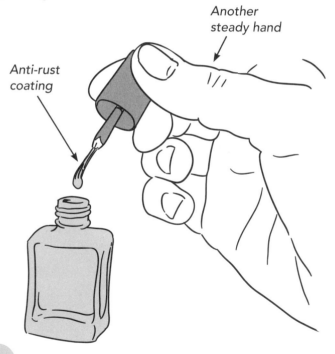

Another
steady hand

Anti-rust
coating

DIY
HACKS

Even a top-notch DIYer can benefit from a short cut here and there, and for a novice, time- and effort-saving tricks can be a godsend. This chapter gives you hacks for everything from painting and screwing to drilling and sharpening, though there's no hack for feeling smug after a job well done.

CUPBOARD SPACE EXPANDER KIT

There's a point for every home owner where space becomes a premium. Maybe your beer bottle collection has grown to ridiculous proportions, or you've reached peak DVD. Well, here's a neat trick to utilise more space in your cupboards.

This only really works for things you can hang up, but if you sort them out that potentially means you've freed up space elsewhere. Get yourself some screw-in hooks and attach them evenly to the upper shelf of your cupboard space. This means you can hang (rather than stack) things like cups, which makes much better use of the space.

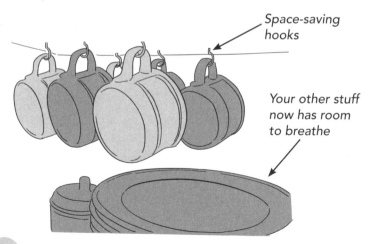

Space-saving hooks

Your other stuff now has room to breathe

CLEVER DRILLING

Drilling a hole in some wood seems pretty straightforward, doesn't it? But, just like many seemingly easy things, there's an art to perfecting it. If you're intent on getting a nice clean hole (no giggling), free from scruffy bits (no giggling!) use this hack.

Slot a piece of scrap wood underneath the piece you're drilling into, and go all the way through to the scrap piece with your drill. That way, the stress of the drilling, which can cause unsightly spiking around the hole, is transferred to the scrap piece.

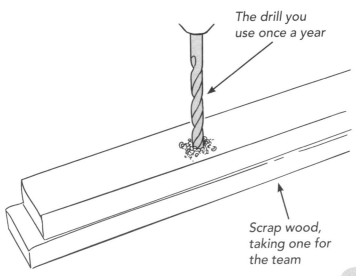

The drill you use once a year

Scrap wood, taking one for the team

THUMB-SAVER

A bruised thumbnail is a mark of shame for the amateur DIYer. How can you miss a nail head with something that is dozens of times bigger? You can, and we've all done it. Here's a way of avoiding it, especially when you're dealing with small, fiddly nails.

Grab a pencil with an eraser on the end, slide the titchy nail into the rubber, point it at your surface and hammer away with your fingers completely clear of the bruising end of the hammer.

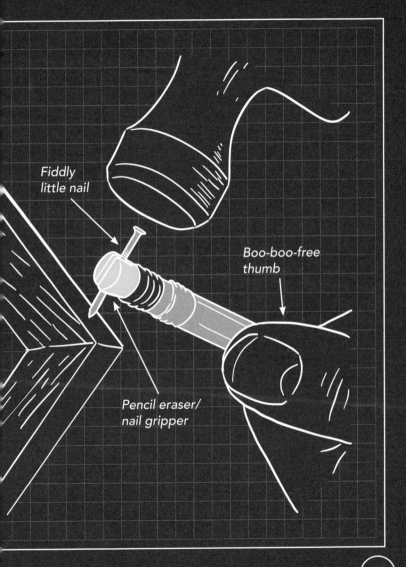

Fiddly little nail

Boo-boo-free thumb

Pencil eraser/ nail gripper

SEASON AND STICK

This hack might seem a little weird, but trust me, it works. Whenever you're gluing one thing to another, you can expect to see some movement - the glue needs time to set, and until then things can slip all over the place. Here's a trick to help prevent this.

Apply glue to the surfaces you want stuck together and lightly press the two pieces together to distribute the glue evenly. Take the two pieces apart again and sprinkle a little table salt over both sticky sides. Then when you stick the two pieces together the friction caused by the salt will stop them from moving. Salted.

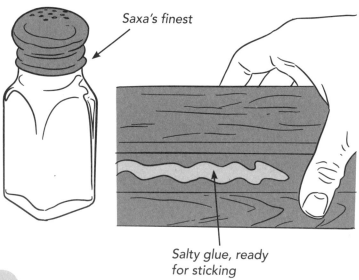

Saxa's finest

Salty glue, ready
for sticking

CERAMIC SHARPENER

Blunt tools – whether in the kitchen or in the workshop – are next to useless, but getting them back to their fully sharpened glory can be complicated. This hack will make things easier.

Take that horrible novelty mug or bowl that you never really use and turn it base-side up. You should see a ring of non-glazed ceramic. This area will be rough enough to sharpen, but soft enough not to blunt, a standard steel blade like the ones used in kitchen knives and other such implements. Angle the blade and slide it back and forth slowly and evenly. Repeat on the other side and you're done. Test your knife on a vegetable – not on your fingers!

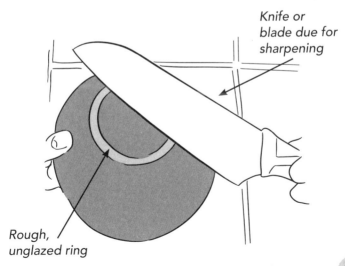

Knife or blade due for sharpening

Rough, unglazed ring

WOOD FILLER

When it comes to DIY, you have those who just want to do the job to an acceptable standard (interpretations of 'acceptable' may vary), and those who want it to be perfect. This woodwork hack is for the latter.

When using wood that has eyes or other unsightly holes, first fill the marks with glue and then sand off some sawdust from a scrap piece of the same kind of wood to fill the void. Leave to dry, sand down and you have a perfectly blended fill.

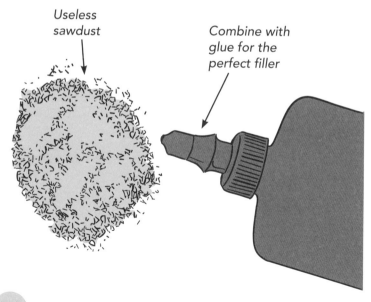

Useless sawdust

Combine with glue for the perfect filler

DEAD-ON DRILLING

If you use power tools all the time then maybe you can do without this hack; for those with a drilling arm made of jelly, listen up.

To drill your hole dead straight, take two pieces of scrap wood (with flat, even ends) and put them next to each other on top of the material you'll be drilling. Stagger the ends so they make a right angle, the corner of which should then be lined up with your hole mark. This right-angle corner will act as a guide and support for when you're drilling, stopping the bit from going wonky and ensuring you get the perfect result.

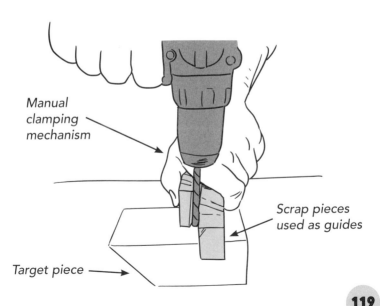

Manual clamping mechanism

Scrap pieces used as guides

Target piece

DRILL DEPTH GAUGE

It's nigh-on impossible to keep track of exactly how far you've drilled into a wall or down into a piece of wood just by watching the bit. Save yourself some time and use this hack to get it right without trying.

Measure the depth you want your hole to be (if you're using a rawl plug, just put it next to the bit) and then mark off this length with a piece of tape on your bit. Get drilling and stop when the tape reaches the surface.

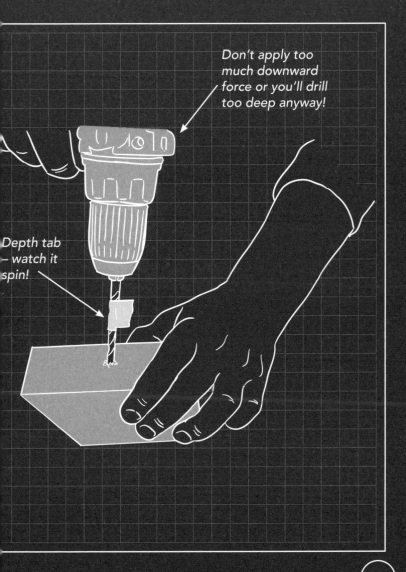

PAINT ROLLER DE-LINTER

Here's another hack for the perfectionist DIYer. Some people would just take their used paint roller and crack on with the next job, but if you want to be sure you're getting the most out of it you'll need to give it a bit of attention before you begin.

Remove any dust, hair, fluff and other paint-spoiling detritus by running a de-lint roller over your paint roller. It will remove crud and perk up the roller material ready for your next masterpiece.

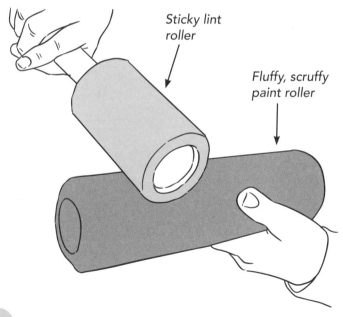

Sticky lint roller

Fluffy, scruffy paint roller

SMALL-SPACE HOOVER

Most DIY activities are going to involve making a mess. The worst is dust from drilling into walls or wood, especially when it gets into small nooks and crannies. This hack will help clean into even the smallest space.

You will need a paper or plastic cup and a drinking straw. Make a hole in the centre of the base of the cup and stick the straw through, fixing it on the inside with some tape, then make a diagonal cut to form a point on the end of the straw. Put the hoover nozzle into the open end of the cup and over the straw – and that's your small-space hoover.

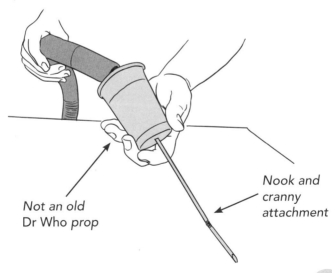

Not an old Dr Who prop

Nook and cranny attachment

WINDOW PAINTING

Prepping for painting can be a real pain. It will usually involve sticking tape in perfect lines to mask awkward areas, and this can get really old really quickly. When it comes to windows with a million panes, it's a nightmare – unless you use this hack.

Save the fiddling and simply use wet newspaper to mask each pane instead. Run a sheet of newspaper under the tap (try not to soak it) and stick it to the window pane; if the newspaper is too large just fold it over and stick, using a little more water.

Peel back to reveal untouched windows

Slips are covered by the paper

SPANNER TIME

Unless you have a tasty collection of spanners (or an adjustable one), you'll most likely grab the paltry one or two in your collection and set to work on your nut or bolt, only to find the spanner is too damn big. Well, next time you do the job be sure to bring your flathead screwdriver too.

If your spanner is too large to grip the head, just wedge your flathead screwdriver in the gap and turn it around along with the spanner.

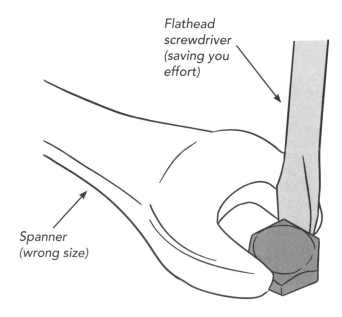

Flathead
screwdriver
(saving you
effort)

Spanner
(wrong size)

NOOK-AND-CRANNY PAINTBRUSH

If you are faced with a tricky area to paint – behind the toilet or radiator, for example – don't jab away at the area with the tip of your brush, risking getting your paint over everything but the wall.

Use a paint pad or sponge and glue it to a stir stick, the kind you usually get free from a paint shop. Dab the sponge with a good layer of paint and get to work on those hard-to-reach areas.

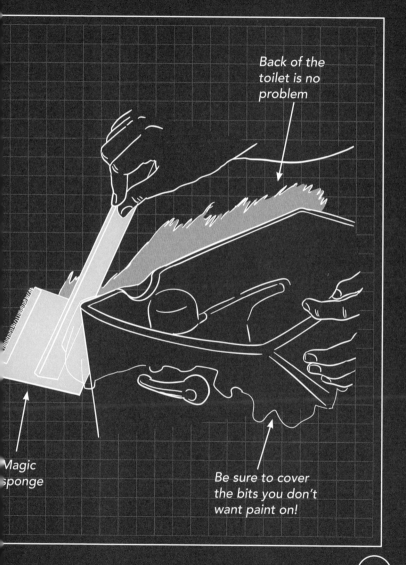

Back of the toilet is no problem

Magic sponge

Be sure to cover the bits you don't want paint on!

COTTON-BUD CORRECTOR

It's annoying when you spend ages preparing to paint, only to find after you're done that there are random marks where the paint has bled through your masking. As long as you spot these minor errors before they dry, you can correct them.

Get yourself a box of cotton buds with the pointy ends, dampen one of the pointed ends with water and proceed to wipe away the errant paint; then use the dry end to finish the job.

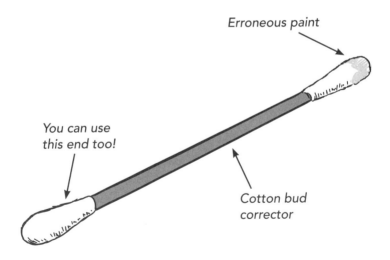

Erroneous paint

You can use this end too!

Cotton bud corrector

PAINTBRUSH CLEAN-UP

You've finally finished painting, so you chuck your brushes back into the shed and forget about them until the next painting job comes up. You may think this is a feasible option, but it isn't.

Cleaning your brushes might sound like an annoying chore, but in fact it's easy. If you're low on turpentine, soak your brushes in hot white vinegar to get rid of drying paint while softening the bristles. Then wash through with warm soapy water. Now you can chuck them in the shed.

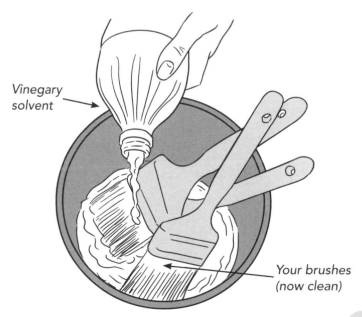

Vinegary solvent

Your brushes (now clean)

KILLER FILLER TECHNIQUE

While hammering a hole sounds counter-intuitive, it's a good idea if you want to do a proper job of covering up holes and dents in walls with filler.

Gently tap the hammer over the hole and keep going until it forms a smooth indentation around it. This will allow the filler to stick much better and more evenly.

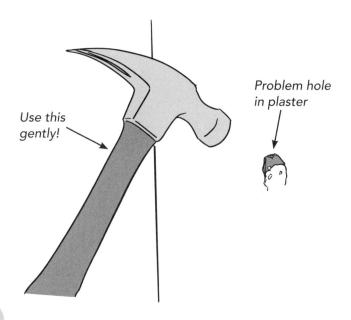

Problem hole in plaster

Use this gently!

RUST AWAY

There will be many points in your life when you have to throw away weird packaging paraphernalia: foam peanuts, polystyrene surrounds, silica gel. You'll want to hold on to the last one, however, for this hack.

Silica gel is not for eating, as the packet always says, but it is for removing moisture in confined spaces. So save that sachet and put it into your toolbox. Your tools will now not be subject to excess moisture and, therefore, rust.

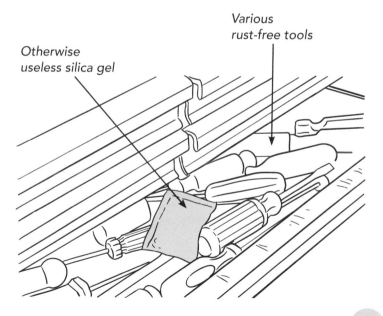

Various rust-free tools

Otherwise useless silica gel

PICTURE NAIL CHEAT

It's always the same conundrum with hanging pictures, isn't it? You need to hold the picture up on the wall to get a position you like, but at the same time you need to mark the wall to know where to put the nails for the fixings on the back. It's impossible to do simultaneously unless you're some kind of stretchy superhuman – or you've read this hack.

Dab toothpaste onto the fixings on the back of the frame, get your picture in place and gently press onto the wall. Lift it off to reveal two small toothpaste markings that will be exactly where you need to bang your nails in.

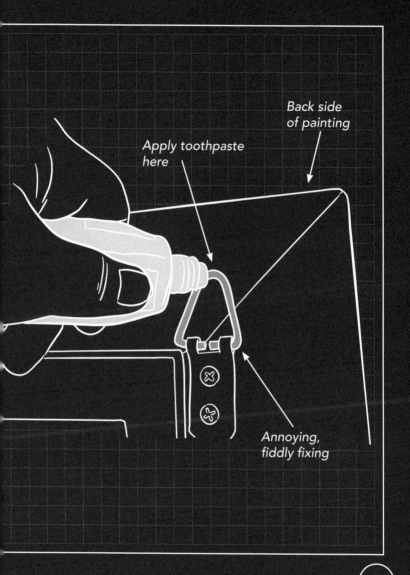

Back side
of painting

Apply toothpaste
here

Annoying,
fiddly fixing

GROOMING HACKS

No, we're not talking about tips on brushing the knots out of your Afghan, we're talking about you! Keeping your hair, skin and other intimate areas in check is nothing to sneer at – it's just sensible. This chapter is packed with ways to make you look and feel better (without using alcohol).

DE-FRIZZ YOUR DO

If you're the kind of guy who likes to keep his do on point (or you have especially unruly hair that looks daft if you don't style it well), you'll appreciate this hack.

On days when there's moisture in the air, your hair can get messed up pretty quickly. If this happens, head for the hand cream. You might have some in the restrooms at work, you might be able to borrow some from a friend or colleague - that part's up to you. Get in front of the mirror and use the hand cream like you would any styling product to shape and tame your hair. It's a quick fix, but will save you from looking scruffy!

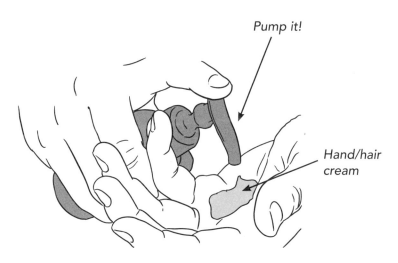

Pump it!

Hand/hair cream

TEA BAG SUNBURN TREATMENT

Whether you're on a lads' holiday in Ibiza or chilling at the local park, sunburn is not something you want to have to deal with. But the lure of the sun is always there, and chances are you'll forget the sun lotion at some point. If you've forgotten the suncream you definitely won't have aftersun – so here's how to soothe yourself.

Use cold tea bags. They're full of tannic acid, which sounds like an irritant but in fact will calm the burnt areas of your skin. Just remember to wash the tea off afterwards!

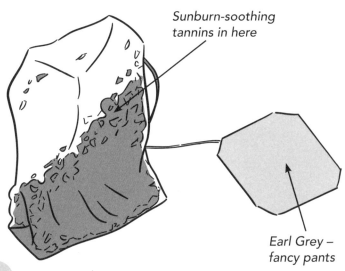

Sunburn-soothing tannins in here

Earl Grey – fancy pants

POST-SHOWER SHAVE

It's totally normal to think shaving *then* showering is the way to do things. It's like getting your hair cut - you want to get rid of those little bits of hair, so you wash after the deed. Just like with a haircut, though, it's usually beneficial to wash your hair right before you get it cut.

Take a shower, then shave. The steam and warm water will soften your facial hair and follicles, making for a smoother, closer trim.

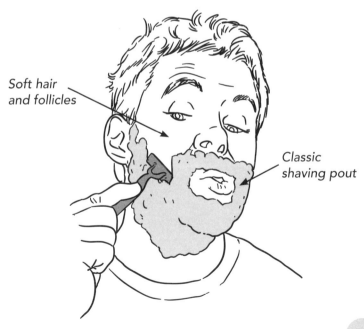

Soft hair and follicles

Classic shaving pout

SCENT EXTENDER

Here's a clever way of making your (most likely ridiculously) expensive aftershave last that much longer.

By adding a touch of petroleum jelly to the pulse point areas where you would usually apply aftershave (before you apply your eau de toilette), you will in effect catch the scent and fix it in place. This is especially useful if you're down to your last bit of Lothario No. 1.

First use a dab of this

Then add a dab of this

PETROLEUM JELLY

EAU DE TOILETTE

NATURAL CONDITIONER

This is another hair-related hack to keep your do on track. You might not be a fan of conditioner (unless your hair is a real pain to look after), but giving it some love before you come to styling is a winner. You needn't use the latest product from the flashiest brands – you can do the job more naturally with aloe vera gel.

Aloe vera is a natural moisturiser and an emollient that will smooth the cuticles of your hair. Apply the gel in the shower as you normally would and work it into the roots. Leave it on for a few minutes and then rinse thoroughly. You will be left with infinitely more manageable hair.

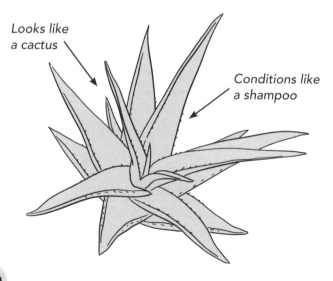

Looks like a cactus

Conditions like a shampoo

PUCKER UP

Using lip balm from a tube is not something every guy can get his head around - maybe because it resembles lipstick! But even if you're cool with lip balm you can still experience dry, chapped lips - not a good look. Here's an easy way to fix them.

Use your toothbrush to scrub your smackers. After you have finished brushing your teeth, use the brush over your lips to dislodge damaged skin and rejuvenate your grinning gear.

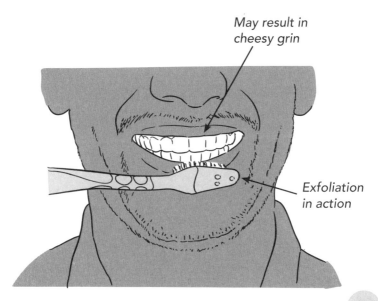

May result in cheesy grin

Exfoliation in action

DON'T WASH YOUR HAIR SO MUCH!

It sounds gross, but the fact is that you probably wash your hair more than you actually need to. Washing hair removes dirt and odour and makes it more manageable, but it also washes away natural oils that benefit your hair and scalp and keep everything in balance. Even notable stylists advocate washing your hair every two to three days rather than once a day. So lose the shampoo for healthier hair and scalp!

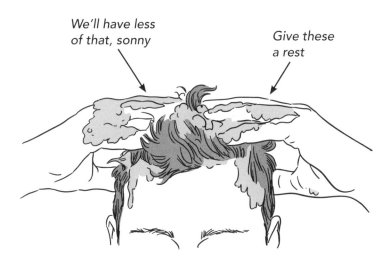

COFFEE FILTER CLEANSER

Coffee filters are great at filtering coffee – but did you know they are also great at cleansing your face? Well, it's true. Now, there are plenty of cleansing-specific products out there for you to spend your hard-earned cash on, but if you're a coffee fan as well as someone who might benefit from a bit of facial TLC, then this hack is for you.

These filters are often light and absorbent, meaning that when pressed against the skin they will lift off any excess oil that might be present – a great substitute for expensive cleansing wipes!

Filters coffee

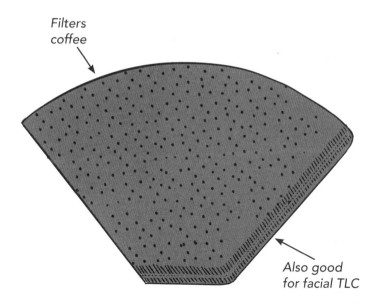

Also good for facial TLC

THE PERFECT CUT

The perfect haircut isn't just about which hairdresser you go to or how much money you pay, nor is it about keeping up with the latest trend. The essential thing is to get a haircut that suits your face shape - it's basic geometry.

If you have a roughly round or square face, you'll want a haircut that makes you look more oval - the most visually appealing shape for a face. So, aim for a cut that has some height to it, and that is short on the sides and longer on top. If you already have an oval face, you'll want to go for something that doesn't add too much length to your face - so, something that's shorter and flatter on top (including long hairstyles).

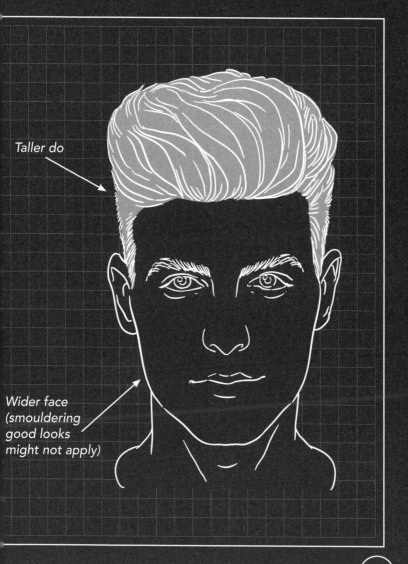

Taller do

Wider face (smouldering good looks might not apply)

SHAVING NICK FIXER

If you happen to cut yourself shaving, don't bother faffing around blotting it with tissue. Try something that will take less time and will clear up instantly.

Lip balm (if you're a fan of the stuff, or petroleum jelly if you're not) is a great way to treat your nicks – especially if you're just about to leave the house.

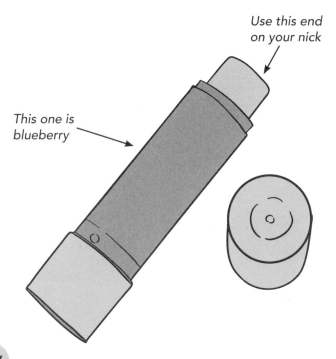

Use this end on your nick

This one is blueberry

GYM BAG DEODORISER

If you actually use the gym (and there are many of us who have a membership but don't actually go!), after a while your gym bag will not smell pretty. Here's a hack to help.

Simply chuck an agreeably scented bar of soap into an old handkerchief (or a small net bag) and place it in your bag. Your bag will now smell of soap, which will be much more pleasant than the musty alternative.

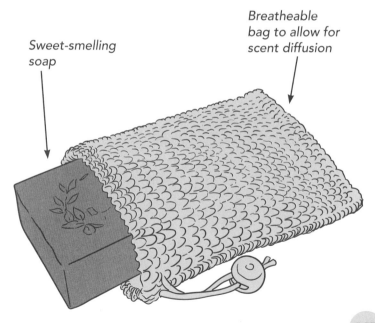

Sweet-smelling soap

Breatheable bag to allow for scent diffusion

FASHION HACKS

You might think you have your style sussed, but when it comes to fashion there is always something new to learn. This chapter combines classic golden rules with some neat tricks to ensure you're looking fly in any situation.

GO FOR GREY

Maybe you haven't worn a vest since your mum made you put one on before sending you off to school, and if so, you're missing out. Vests are an old-school way of keeping warm when dressing smart. However, there's one thing to keep in mind – white underwear is always a no-go, so choose grey.

Anything worn next to the body will be subject to discoloration from sweat, but this will be less obvious on grey. Also, grey vests will show up less underneath a white shirt than white. (Don't believe me? Try it!)

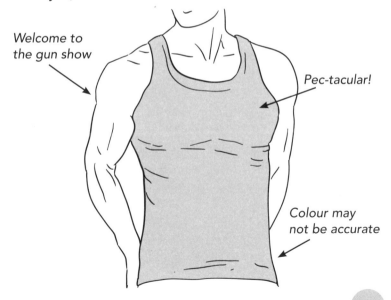

Welcome to the gun show

Pec-tacular!

Colour may not be accurate

THE PINCH AND TUCK TECHNIQUE

Excess shirt material hanging over the top of your trousers is not a good look. Nowadays many shirts come tailored for a close fit, but you might have some older ones in your wardrobe that are more generously cut. Here's a hack to get them looking tidy.

Grab your shirt either side of your hips, at the end of the long seams running down the sides. Pinch the seams between forefinger and thumb and fold them back onto themselves, as if you're trying to make the waist fit of the shirt smaller. Now tuck them in and you will have eliminated any excess material from peeping out above your trousers.

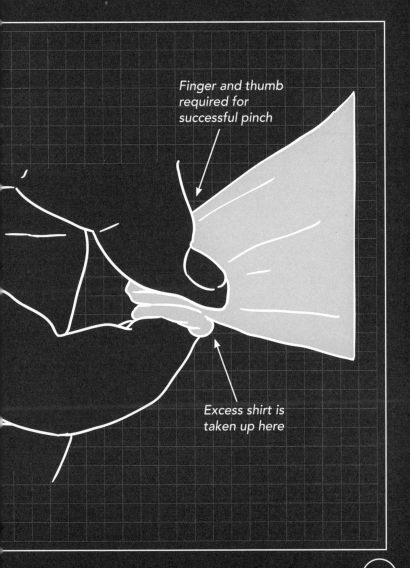

Finger and thumb required for successful pinch

Excess shirt is taken up here

HUES FOR YOU

Did you know that style is in your genes? No, we're not talking about good cheekbones or glossy hair, we're talking about skin tone. As well as choosing clothes that fit properly and look stylish, spare a thought for how the colour goes with your skin tone.

The key is contrast – if you've got fair skin try wearing racing green, burgundy, dark grey and navy, and avoid pastels or bright colours. Men with olive skin should steer clear of neutrals and opt for darker shades, while those with darker skin tones are lucky enough to suit most clothing colours – just avoid the shades too similar to your own skin tone.

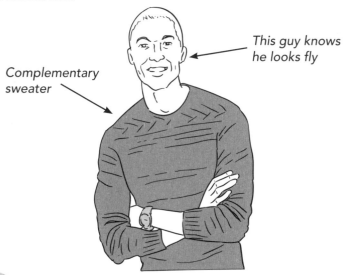

This guy knows he looks fly

Complementary sweater

SUIT SHOULDER TRICK

One of the ugliest sights at any formal gathering is a man in an ill-fitting suit (times two if the guy is horribly drunk). If you're buying off the rack, however, it's easy to fall into the trap of getting a jacket that's too big, so here's how to check.

Put the jacket on and stand sideways on next to a wall. Then lean into the wall slowly. If the shoulder pad scrunches up before your shoulder touches the wall the jacket is too big. You are aiming for your shoulder to hit the wall the exact same time the jacket shoulder pad does, and when this happens you will have found the perfect suit jacket.

'I wonder what's for dinner' face

Look for bunching here

THE HANDSHAKE TEST

Here's part two of your off-the-rack suit-size check. An ill-fitting suit can also reveal itself around the armholes, so use this technique to test them.

Hold your arm out in front of a mirror in the handshake position. If the jacket moves upwards and buckles just underneath the shoulder pad, then you know that you should get a different size (or brand) – look for higher arm holes.

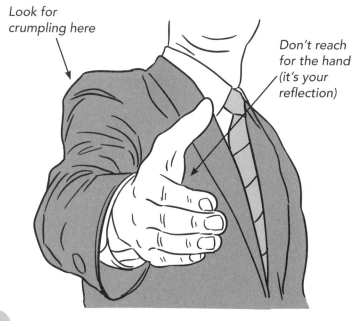

Look for crumpling here

Don't reach for the hand (it's your reflection)

DE-LINT YOUR DUDS

If you're a smart son of a gun and a veteran suit wearer, you might already own a lint brush. For those of you who don't, this is Hacks' way to de-lint and de-hair your clothes.

Take some sticky tape, find the end and then proceed to wrap it around your outstretched hand, sticky side out, covering your fingers but not your thumb. Once you've reached the ends of your fingers, cut the tape off. Your hand has now been transformed into a pet hair-removing, lint-grabbing instrument – simply press down onto the affected areas.

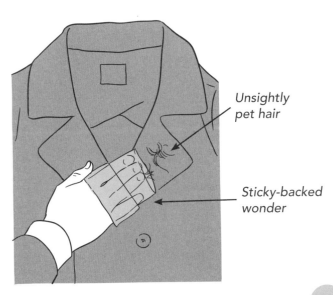

Unsightly pet hair

Sticky-backed wonder

ON A ROLL

Rolling up your shirt sleeves is something you probably don't even think about. There's nothing to it - you fold the sleeve back on itself until it's short enough and you're done. But have you ever noticed how sleeves can unroll themselves? Seriously annoying, especially if you're working with your hands. Here's a better way.

Step one: hold your arm out and unbutton the sleeve. Flip the cuff over towards you. Step two: pull the folded cuff further up to your elbow. Step three: flip the excess material over to fasten for the perfectly folded sleeve.

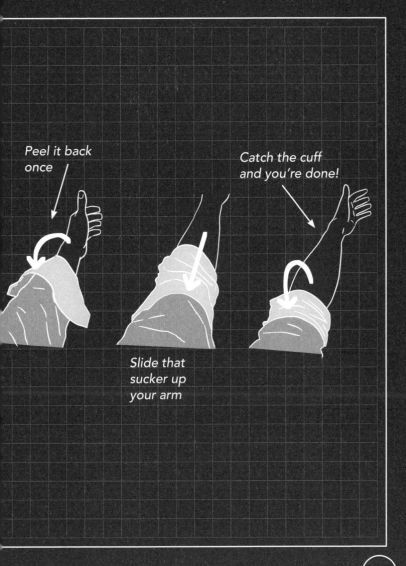

SNAP TAG

Always forget your size when stocking up on your favourite denim? Or maybe you want to check if your favourite brand is still manufacturing that old Oxford shirt? Here's a hack to help you track down your favourite gear when it comes to replacing it.

Whenever you find something you like and that fits you perfectly, take a quick snap of the label on your smartphone and save the shots in an album for future reference.

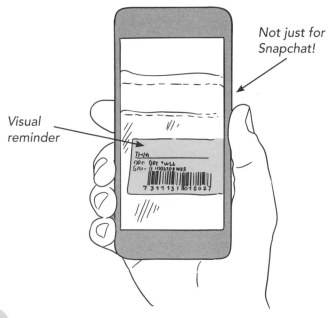

Not just for Snapchat!

Visual reminder

SALT SHOE SCRUB

If you own a pair (or many pairs) of shoes that you really care about, you'll want to keep them looking good for as long as you can. Cleaning and polishing shouldn't be a major issue, except when it comes to more stubborn stains like those caused by salt. You might pick up stains like this in winter when walkways are treated with salt, and they can be tough to shift.

The solution (no pun intended) is white vinegar. Apply a little to the affected area and then use an old toothbrush to lift the unsightly stain away.

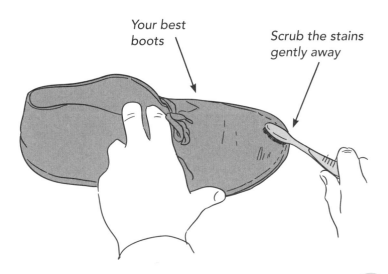

Your best boots

Scrub the stains gently away

THE PERFECT SUNGLASSES

The supreme shades are out there somewhere; the trick is just to match them to your face shape.

So, if you have a round face, go for angular shades, some Wayfarers or square frames to give your face definition. An oval face will look good with a round pair of frames that are as wide as the widest part of your face, while a square face will benefit from slightly curved frames to soften the edges. A triangular face will need top-heavy frames to balance your face shape.

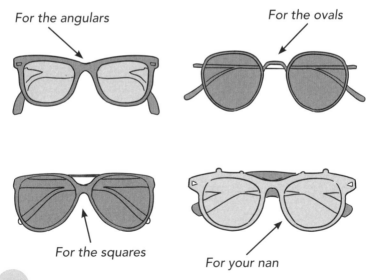

For the angulars

For the ovals

For the squares

For your nan

GADGET HACKS

You don't have to be a geek to enjoy a gadget – smartphones and tablets are everywhere, and with them come endless opportunities for new hacks. This chapter will help you get the best out of your hi-tech gear as well as give you some low-tech cheats for things that are a little less sophisticated – AAA batteries anyone?

BATTERY BODGE

Remember batteries? Those small metal cylindrical things you used to have to put into electrical things to make them work? Well hopefully you do, because plenty of things still require them. And do you remember how annoying it is to not have them when you need them? Here's a hack to help.

If you're in need of AA batteries and all you can find are AAAs you can make them fit. Place the batteries in the battery compartment and use a wad of tin foil as an extension on the positive node (don't try to use the other end, as the spring will mess it all up).

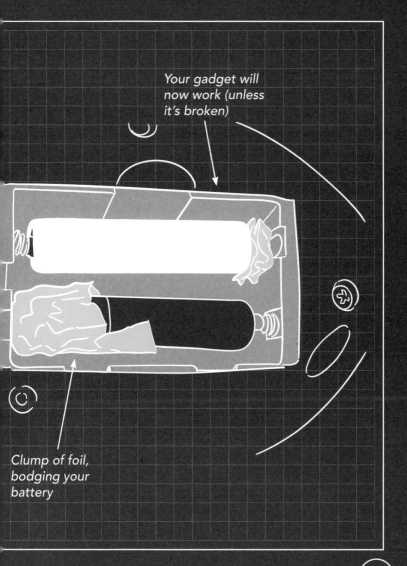

Your gadget will now work (unless it's broken)

Clump of foil, bodging your battery

AMP UP YOUR WIFI

Experts will tell you that beer and electrical equipment don't mix, but what do they know? When it comes to wifi it can definitely help. No, we're not talking about getting drunk and watching cat videos, we're talking signal boosting.

Take a can of your favourite beer (soft drinks are also acceptable) and dutifully drink it. Rinse out and dry the can, then fetch your strongest scissors. Pierce the can midway down and cut in a line up to the top, then down to the bottom. Next, cut around the rim of the can at the bottom and remove it entirely. Cut around the rim at the top, leaving an inch so you don't cut the whole thing off. Spread the can out to create wings, and place it on your router aerial. Say hello to an improved wifi signal.

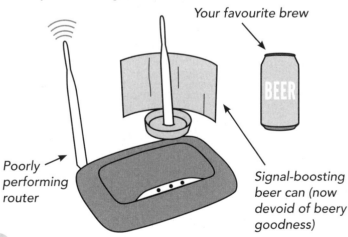

Your favourite brew

BEER

Poorly performing router

Signal-boosting beer can (now devoid of beery goodness)

HEADPHONE CADDY

No gadget user is more deserving of sympathy than the poor wretch who suffers that most soul-destroying of predicaments: headphone tangle. Just how in the name of Steve Jobs do they get so damn knotted?! Worry not, child – there is hope for redemption in the form of this hack.

Take an old credit/debit card (everybody has one in a drawer somewhere) and drill two holes about 5mm across at either end (positioned along the centre line of the card). Next, grab some scissors and cut in at a 45-degree angle at all corners of the card, then proceed to join the cuts along the longest edges. To utilise your headphone caddy, thread the jack end through one hole and pull through, wrap the wire around the body of the card and finally thread the jack end into the hole at the other end.

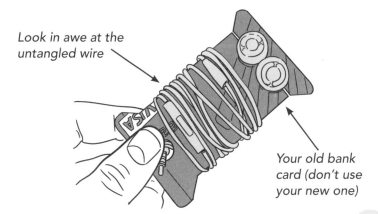

Look in awe at the untangled wire

Your old bank card (don't use your new one)

HD VIEWING

If you want to view your online cat videos in HD using that best-known of all video websites but can't find the option for it, then all you need are a few not-so-secret codes to make it happen.

To unlock the HD options all you need to do is add a code to the end of your URL. Put in **&fmt=18** to get stereo sounds and 480x270 resolution, and add **&fmt=22** to get 1280x720 resolution instead.

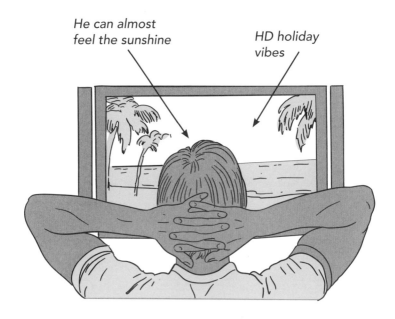

He can almost feel the sunshine

HD holiday vibes

TABLET CASE

If you don't have a case for your tablet, or you're security conscious and like the idea of concealing it from prying eyes, this hack is for you.

You can turn a regular notebook into a tablet cover in a few easy steps. First, find a notebook slightly bigger than your tablet, preferably with a strong, rigid cover, and carefully remove half of the pages. Next, source some elastic – you can buy it in rolls from any craft store – and cut four 2-inch lengths. Grab your scissors and pierce the back cover, making two holes about an inch apart in each corner. Thread your lengths of elastic through the holes from inside to outside to create loops on the inside of the notebook, and tie knots in the loose ends to stop them coming back through. You now have a notebook-cum-tablet cover with loops to hold the corners of your gadget in place.

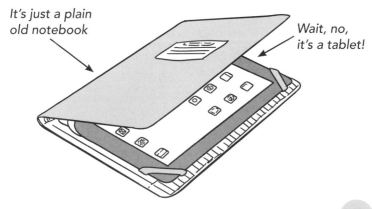

It's just a plain old notebook

Wait, no, it's a tablet!

SPEC-TACULAR PHONE STAND

This one is so simple it's stupid. Whether you wear shades or prescription glasses you can create a mini smartphone stand, for when you're on a train or plane and you want to watch a video of some kind, within seconds.

Step 1: remove glasses, fold the arms in and place them onto a flat surface upside down, with the arms facing towards you.

Step 2: rest your phone on the folded arms and hit play. You are now watching content on your phone without having to hold it. Just be aware that if you're long-sighted you might need your glasses to see your screen.

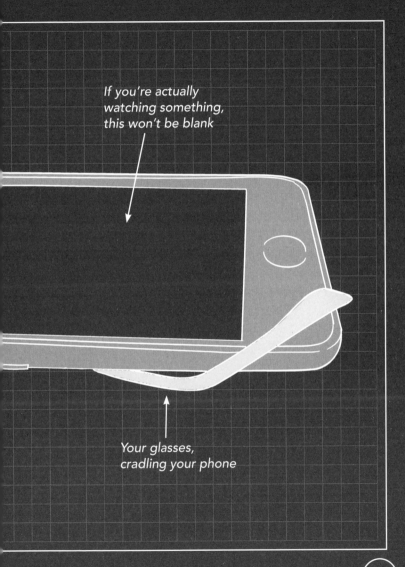

If you're actually watching something, this won't be blank

Your glasses, cradling your phone

169

SLIDESHOW SMART

If you really want to go all out on your next presentation make sure that your audience doesn't have to see you faff around pressing every button possible on your keyboard to get a full-screen viewing experience. Be prepared and go in cool-headed knowing your PowerPoint will stun straight away because you have already saved it in show mode.

In the File menu, click Save As, name it, and in the dropdown menu below select PowerPoint Show (PPS) and click Save.

This guy knows his game is on lock

PPS prep, paying off

AUDIO EQUALISER

Whatever you use your smartphone for, other than making calls, is entirely your own business – but I'm willing to bet you use it to listen to music at least some of the time. If so, you'll appreciate this hack.

Go to your app store and search for 'audio equalizer' (whether you spell it with a 'z' or an 's' it should appear). This will help you get the most out of the audio coming from your phone, which, if you're a muso, will be music to your ears.

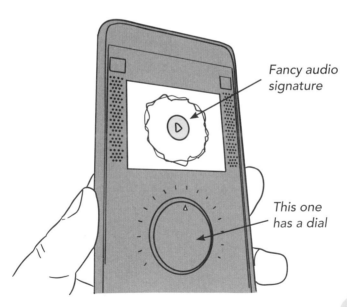

Fancy audio
signature

This one
has a dial

EARPHONE SELFIES

Selfies are now a part of everyday life – there's nothing odd about putting your phone on the end of a stick and taking a photo of yourself. But the selfie stick isn't the only way of making that all-important shot easier to get.

Here's a tip that you might not be aware of. A certain fruit-themed phone brand has made selfie shooting even easier by allowing you to take the shot with the toggle on the headphones, meaning you can use both hands and avoid stretching your thumb awkwardly to the shutter button.

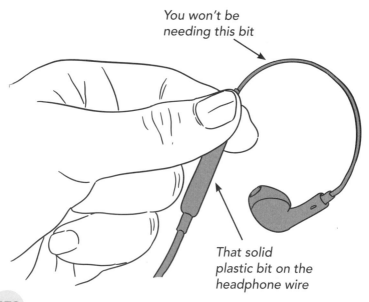

You won't be needing this bit

That solid plastic bit on the headphone wire

MAKESHIFT MIC STAND

Are you an aspiring *X Factor* contestant? A karaoke addict? Or maybe even a proper singer or musician? Even if you're none of the above you will still benefit from this hack, which turns an old wire coat-hanger into a tech stand.

You'll need an old coat-hanger of course, and that's about it! Then you just need to bend it into shape. Make a small bend upwards in the hanger in the middle of the longest edge, so you have an arrow shape, then push the bend away from you until the longest edge is at right angles to the other two edges. This is your basic stand shape. Then, if you're planning on slotting a microphone in there, simply curl the hook over to form a closed circle narrower than the head of your mic. The hook can be shaped to hold various other things, but you can figure that out yourself!

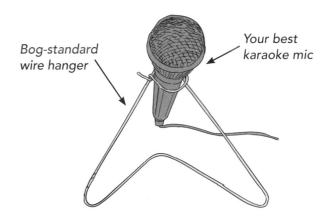

Bog-standard wire hanger

Your best karaoke mic

LAZY SCROLLING

Fed up with the annoying noise your mouse wheel makes or how slow the scrolling is? Or perhaps you just want a cool shortcut for paging up and down when using webpages? We've got you covered.

Use your keyboard to page down by pressing the space bar - and press Shift + space to page up. No more squeaks and finger cramps!

C

Various bits of
detritus (eww)

G H J K

V B N M

In case you didn't know,
the big arrow above
shows the location of
the space bar

SMARTPHONE CLEAN-UP

Sensible smartphone owners will have invested in some sort of case to protect their gadget, but despite the fact that a case will stop your phone from exploding when you drop it, it will also act as a major magnet for dust, lint and grime, which then transfers to the nice, shiny surface of your phone – usually the back. So when you come to take the case off, you've got a gross layer of dirt on your phone. Here's how to clean it.

Grab some toothpaste, squidge a bit out onto the back of your phone and scrub lightly with a paper towel. Use a slightly dampened paper towel to remove the paste, then polish it up with a duster. Your phone will look like new!

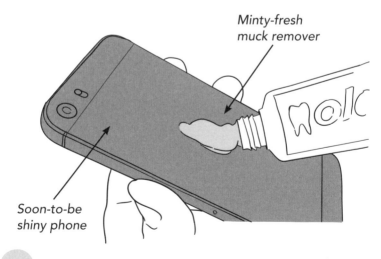

Minty-fresh muck remover

Soon-to-be shiny phone

SURVIVAL HACKS

The great outdoors can be perilous for those who are unprepared. The worst-case-scenario hacks in this chapter might seem a little far-fetched, but you won't be saying that when you're stranded in the woods with only your wits and a ring-pull fishing hook for survival. If you're just spending a few nights at a campsite, you'll probably be fine without them.

NB – in this, of all chapters in the book, reader discretion is advised (you basically want to hope you never have to use any of these hacks).

SUPERGLUE STITCHES

Picture the scene: you and your team have been dropped into the jungle to search for survivors of a helicopter crash, only to find yourself being pursued by a murderous, chameleonic alien. No, wait, that's the plot of *Predator*. Anyway, imagine you're in the middle of nowhere and, like Arnie, you've got a few serious grazes for whatever reason. You have to treat your wounds yourself or you'll bleed to death. What do you do? Reach for the glue!

Superglue, that is. As you might know if you've ever used it before, it sticks skin to skin, so it can be utilised to 'stitch' cuts. Just don't get any *in* the cut, or you'll be hollering like the Predator itself!

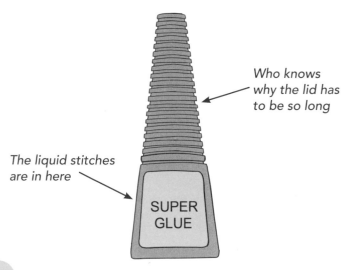

Who knows why the lid has to be so long

The liquid stitches are in here

SUPER GLUE

RING-PULL
FISHING HOOK

If you're caught in the wild you'll need to be able to find food. Depending on how many episodes of Bear Grylls you've watched, you might already have some ideas, but chances are this hack will give you a much more palatable option.

For this you'll need pliers, a drinks can, a length of twine (or other stronger line) and a water source with fish in it. Remove the ring pull from your can and mark out three lines – one bisecting the top edge and two more bisecting the 'bridge' part of the ring pull (see diagram 1). Cut along these lines with your pliers to make your basic hook shape (see diagram 2) then pinch the sharp end to make it more hook-like. Then all you need to do is tie her on, bait her up and get fishing!

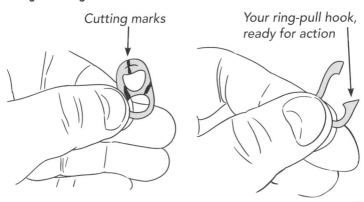

Cutting marks

Your ring-pull hook, ready for action

PORTABLE WHOLEGRAINS

A good outdoorsman will think ahead and take emergency supplies with him. Here's a hack for packing up your pulses.

Why pulses? Well, grains (rice, oats and so on) and pulses (beans) pack a lot of energy, have a long shelf life and are easy to portion out, so they're pretty much the ideal emergency survival food. The ideal way of storing and transporting them is in plastic bottles - they're easily stowed away, light and resilient. So next time you head for the unknown, remember your bottle of rice!

Plastic bottles (aka portable seed silos)

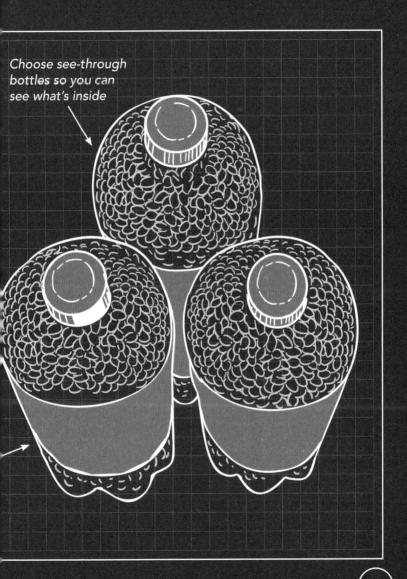

Choose see-through bottles so you can see what's inside

PORTABLE BBQ

Here's another hack that promotes the ethos 'be prepared'. This one is less Ray Mears and more Jamie Oliver, but nonetheless it will help you out when you're short on fire-making materials.

Pack yourself an eggbox full of charcoal and firelighters to create an instant fire for cooking. You don't even need to unpack the combustibles, just light the whole thing up and it will soon settle down into a nicely arranged BBQ-like set-up.

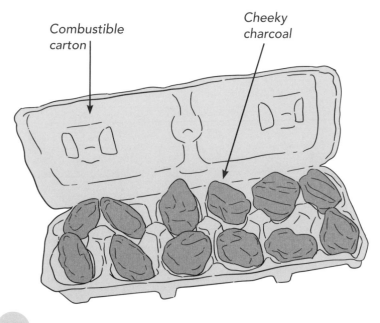

Combustible carton

Cheeky charcoal

X MARKS THE SPOT

We're not talking about treasure here but we are talking about something precious - navigational mastery. When venturing out into dense wilderness you should always carry around a stick of chalk for marking where you have been before.

Apply Xs to trees and other noticeable spots to indicate where you've passed by already, hopefully assisting in your not getting lost! It's an oldie, but a goodie.

It marks the spot!

BATTERY BURNER

Here's another way of making trash into something that will help you live a little longer. For this hack you'll need a chewing gum wrapper – the shiny metallic kind – and an AA battery. Both of these items are easy to bring along on any outdoors trip and this hack shows you how they can make fire.

It's really quite simple: tear off two thin strips of the shiny wrapper, place one at each end of the battery, shiny side down, and bend the free ends over, so they are not near your fingers. Within a short time you will see the free ends of the wrappers burst into flame.

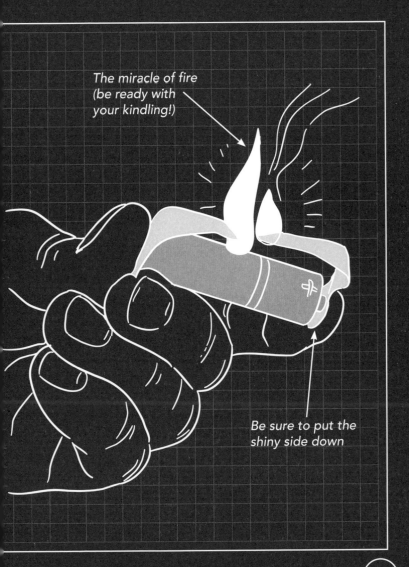

The miracle of fire (be ready with your kindling!)

Be sure to put the shiny side down

HYDRATION ROD

OK, this is less of a hack and more of a stick, but, like the saying goes, it's how you use it that counts.

Staying hydrated in the wilderness is essential in the art of survival so you'll want to make sure that you have enough water to drink. If you've got a long way to walk you won't want to be making multiple trips so to save time, take a long, strong stick and use it to carry multiple water canisters all at the same time.

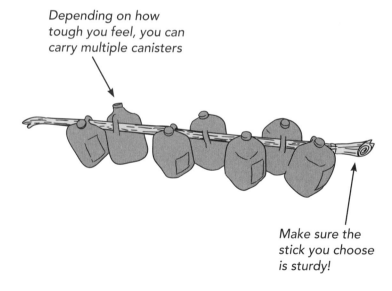

Depending on how tough you feel, you can carry multiple canisters

Make sure the stick you choose is sturdy!

RUBBISH SACK
SURVIVAL MAC

OK, I'll admit it – this hack is a bit rubbish (see what I did there?). But not so much that it is totally useless. It's basically making an emergency rain mac from a rubbish bag, and here's how to do it.

Take one corner of the sack and make a hole big enough to fit your face, then make another two holes just below on either side for your arms and slip this little number on. There you have your lightweight, fully packable, rainproof covering. Who needs Gore-Tex?

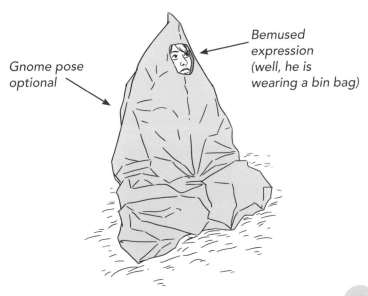

Gnome pose optional

Bemused expression (well, he is wearing a bin bag)

FINAL WORD

Congratulations – you are officially a Man Hack Maestro! You can now go about your manly business safe in the knowledge that you've got the skills to pay the bills (and possibly even save up for that new cordless strimmer you've had your eye on for months).

If you have a hack of your own that you think is worthy of publication, you can send it to us at auntie@summersdale.com.

HACKS INDEX

GROOMING HACKS

FASHION HACKS

GADGET HACKS

SURVIVAL HACKS

If you're interested in finding out more about
our books, find us on Facebook at
Summersdale Publishers
and follow us on Twitter at
@Summersdale.

WWW.SUMMERSDALE.COM